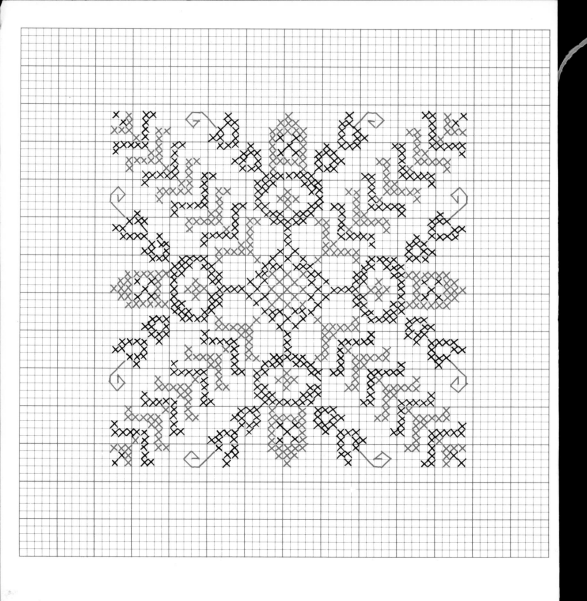

Traditional Motifs
For Needlework
And Knitting

Carola Förg

Lark Books
Asheville, North Carolina

English-language edition
First published in 1992 in the
United States of America by
Lark Books
50 College Street, Asheville NC 28801
ISBN 0-937274-65-8

Library of Congress Cataloging-in-Publication Data
Förg, Carola

      (Altdeutsche Leinenstickerel. English)
      Traditional motifs for needlework and knitting / Carola Förg.
        p.   cm.
      Rev. translation of : Altdeutsche Leinenstickerel.
      ISBN 0-937274-65-8
      1. Embroidery--Europe--Patterns. 2. Decoration and ornament-
-Plant forms. I. Title.
TT769.E85F6713 1992
  746.44'041--dc20   91-44069
                                   CIP

English translation © 1992 Lark Books

and first published in Great Britain in 1992 by
A & C Black (Publishers) Limited
35 Bedford Row, London WC1R 4JH
ISBN 0-7136-3579-7

A CIP catalogue record for this book
is available from the British Library.

©1985 Rosenheimer Verlagshaus
First published in Germany in two volumes
under the title Altdeutsche Leinenstickerei
By Rosenheimer Verlagshaus Alfred Förg GmbH & Co. KG
Rosenheim

Printed in Hong Kong.

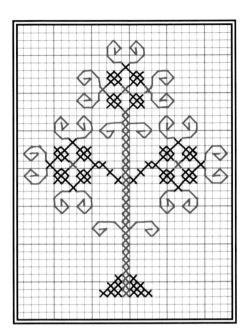

FOREWORD

Needleworkers of all types will delight at this collection of more than 250 original linen embroidery patterns dating back primarily to the 15th, 16th and 17th centuries. (Some patterns date as far back as the Middle Ages.) These patterns, which originated in Germany, France, Italy, Spain, England, Russia, and Roumania, were first published as a collection in 1878 by the collection's director at the German Trade Museum in Berlin and included patterns that had been published separately under the titles *Form oder Modelbüchlein* (Form or Pattern Booklet) in 1523 and *Schönes Neues Modelbunch* (The Beautiful New Pattern Book) in 1597.

The patterns themselves were collected from a wide range of sources: from illustrations copied from popular paintings of the time, from the first printed pattern books published in the late 1500s, and antique samplers that had been handed down through generations of families. (These samplers, called "pattern cloth" by German embroiderers, were used to train needleworkers and preserve patterns and can still be found in museums today.)

Pattern motifs range from floral bouquets, to single blooms, trees, and geometrics. You'll also find several patterns of royal heritage, including the collar pattern worn by Henry VIII's queen, Jane Seymour (copied from a portrait). Single patterns can be used by themselves as a small accent on a project or joined together in any combination you choose on larger projects. Although these patterns were originally done in only one or two colors because of color fading troubles, you should feel free to use as many colors as you desire.

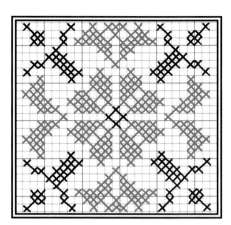

INTRODUCTION

>< >< ><

To duplicate the embroidery patterns shown in this book, it is not necessary to know more than a few of the most popular basic stitches.

Cross Stitch

>< >< ><

Cross stitch is one of the easiest forms of embroidery used in European peasant motifs which are often seen in a restricted color scheme of bold black and red designs.

Evenweave fabrics of linen, cotton or canvas are most common. These are woven with the same weight of thread in either direction and the spaces between warp and weft are square. A single thread makes the best effect. The cross stitch should be bold, but should not crowd its neighbor. The thickness of the thread should be chosen to suit the weight of the fabric. A small blunt tapestry needle should be used to avoid splitting the fabric threads.

Basic Cross Stitch

>< >< ><

Usually worked in rows. Work from right to left, laying down half the crosses, then back from left to right. If you prefer, you can work one cross at a time.

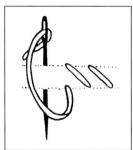
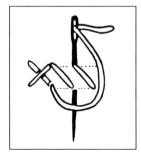

Double Cross Stitch

>< >< ><

This stitch can fill an area or serve as a border. Bring the needle out to the right side and take a diagonal stitch. Bring the needle out directly below end of stitch and take another diagonal stitch across center of first diagonal. Bring the needle out at mid-point of two lower points of star, and cross center. Complete star by bringing the needle out at side midpoint, then crossing center. The result should be a star contained in a perfect square.

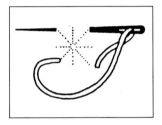 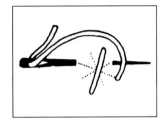 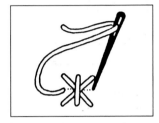

Back Stitch

>< >< ><

This is a common outline stitch. Bring needle to right side along design line, take a small stitch backward, and bring needle to right side again in front of the first stitch, a stitch length away. Continue along the design line, always finishing stitch by inserting needle at point where last stitch began.

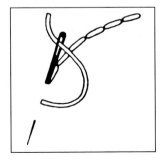

Basic Running Stitch

>< >< ><

Bring the needle to the right side and work from right to left, picking up the same number of threads for each stitch. If the fabric isn't too heavy, you can pick up several stitches on the needle before the thread is pulled through.

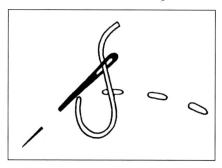

Double Running Stitch

>< >< ><

Like the basic running stitch, this stitch is used for outlining. It consists of two passes of running stitch, one on top of the other. First work evenly spaced running stitches, then turn the fabric over and work a second time, so that the stitches fill in the gaps left by the first pass.

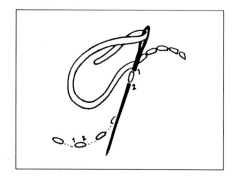

Knitting or
Cross Stitching
on Knitted Fabric

>< >< ><

The charts in this book can be used for knitting in the designs or by cross stitch embroidering over knitted fabric. In both cases, the charts require some adaption, however, since most knitted fabric has fewer stitches in width than in height, using the knitted stitches as a grid will cause a distortion in the look of the design. For example, a typical four-inch swatch of knitting may be 18 stitches in width and 24 rows in height. This means that each stitch will be 25 percent wider than tall. To duplicate the original proportion of a cross stitch chart, look for a knitted fabric or pattern with a gauge with the least difference between height and width.

When knitting from a cross stitch chart, some basic rules of fairisle knitting should be kept in mind. First, there should only be two colors knit in each row. If there are more than two colors, the additional colors should be added later by duplicate or cross stitch, unless you are willing to risk tangled yarn at the back of the work. When knitting the first color, carry the unused color loosely across the wrong side of the work. Be sure to maintain a loose tension or the stitches will be puckered. Knitting a sample first is a good idea to be sure that the proportions of height to width are pleasing to the eye.

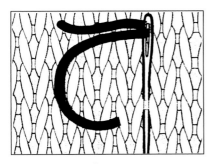

> Step 1 <
Cross Stitch

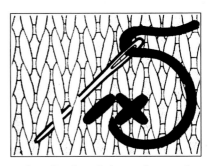

Cross Stitch worked upper horizontal
strand only.

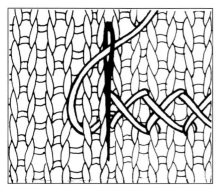 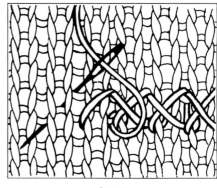

*Step 1 >< Cross Stitch Embroidery over upper
and lower horizontal strand.*

> Step 2 <

To cross stitch over a knitted stitch, follow the illustrations. Each stitch crosses diagonally over a knitted stitch and two diagonal stitches form the cross. If you stitch over the upper and lower horizontal strands, the embroidered stitch will have the same proportions of the knitted stitch and is a suitable method if the stitch and row gauge are very similar. If the proportion of height to width is uneven, embroider over the upper horizontal strand only. You should make a practice swatch to see which way works best.

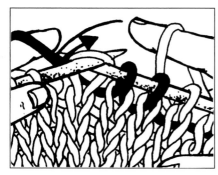 

*Knitting with right hand,
stranding with left.*

*Purling with right hand,
stranding with left.*

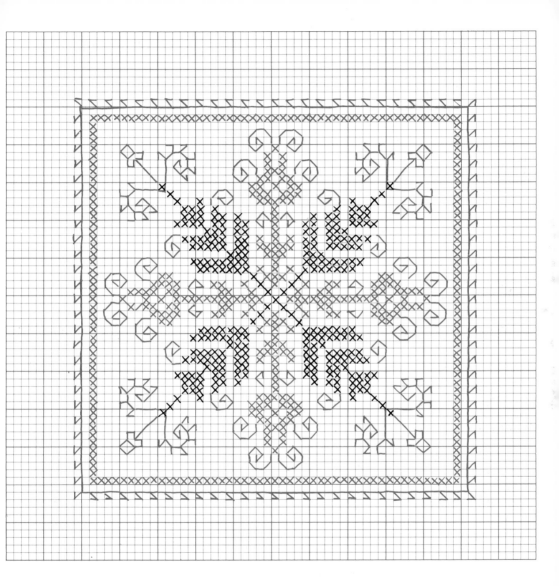

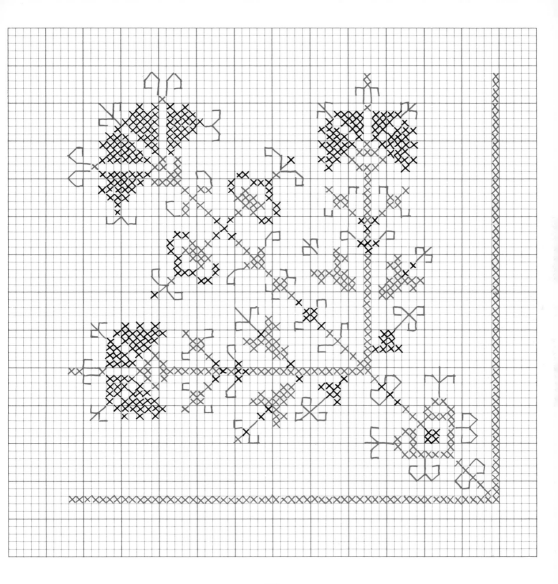

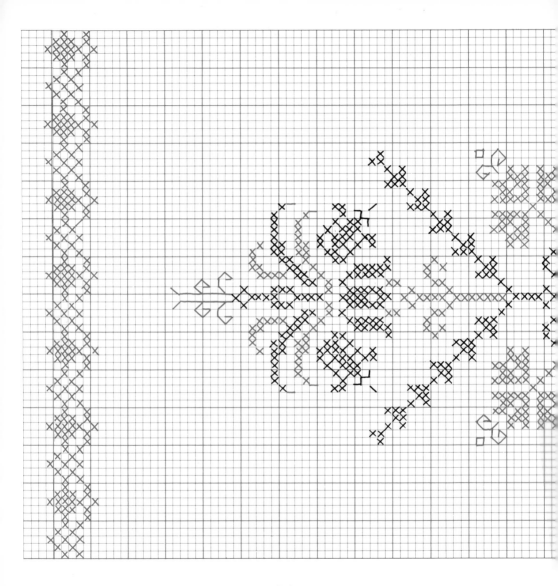

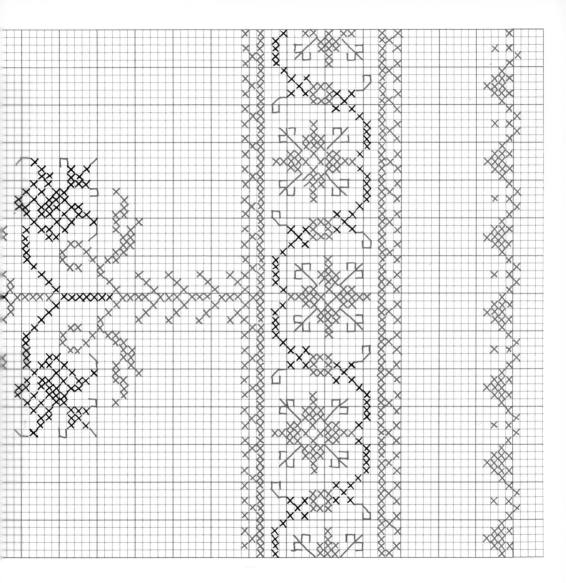

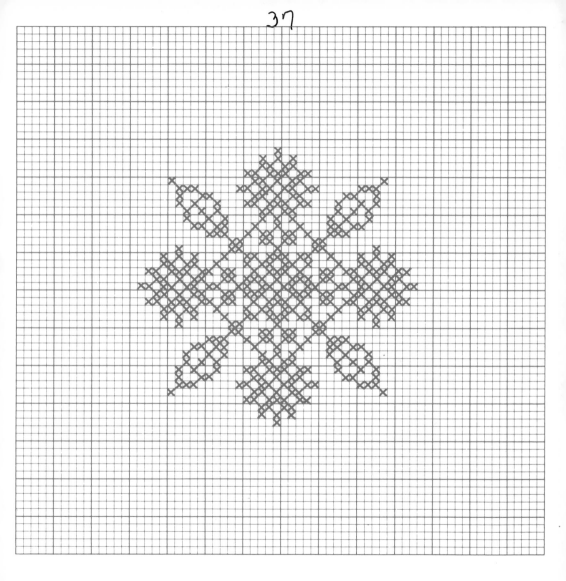

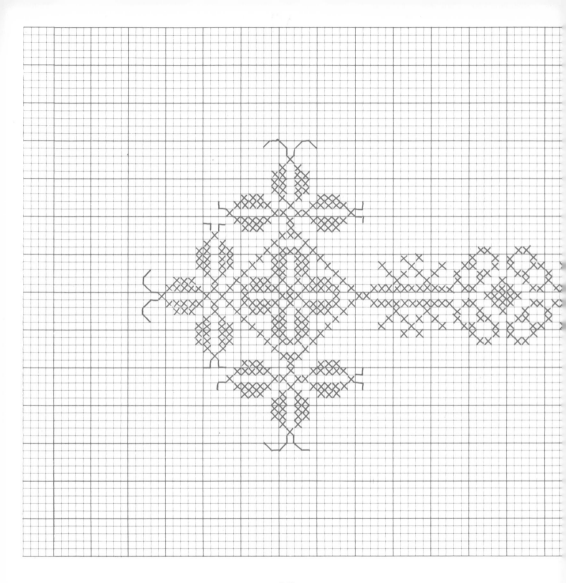

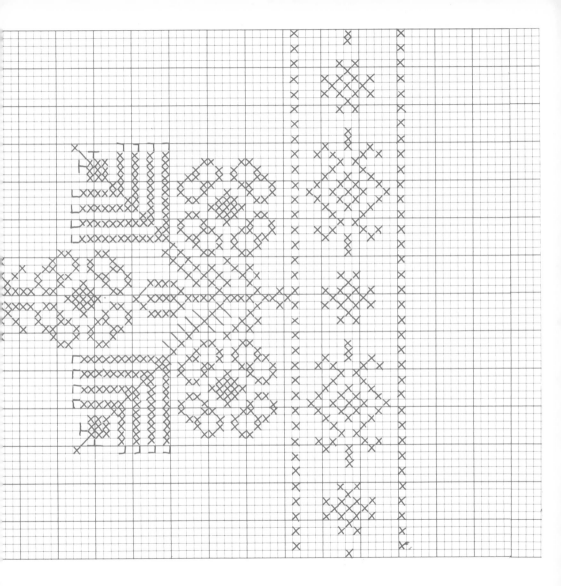

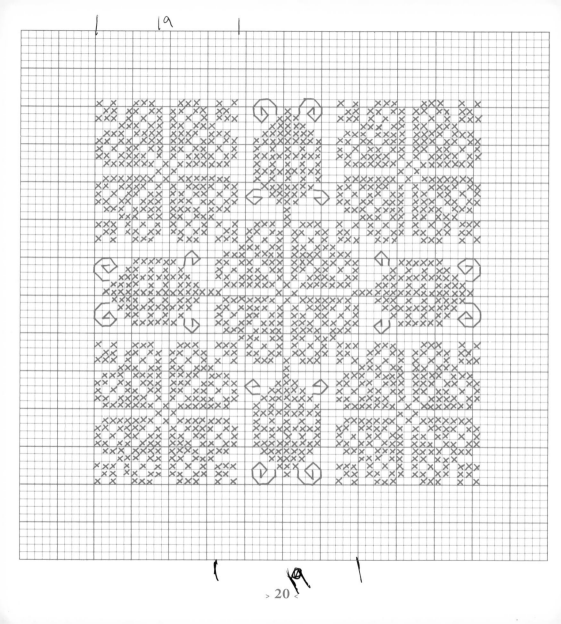

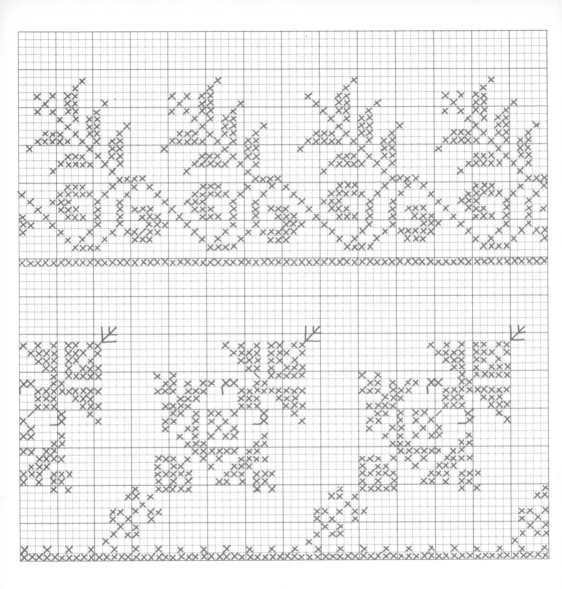

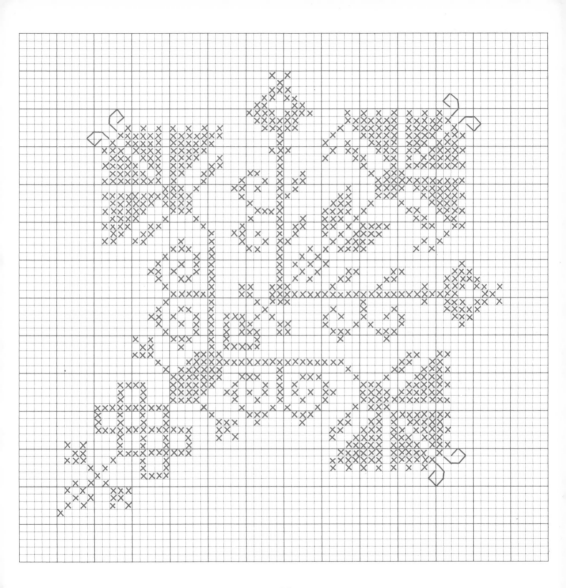

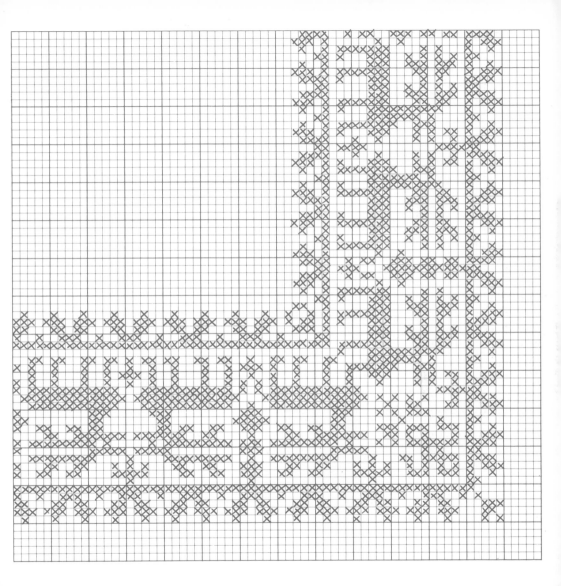

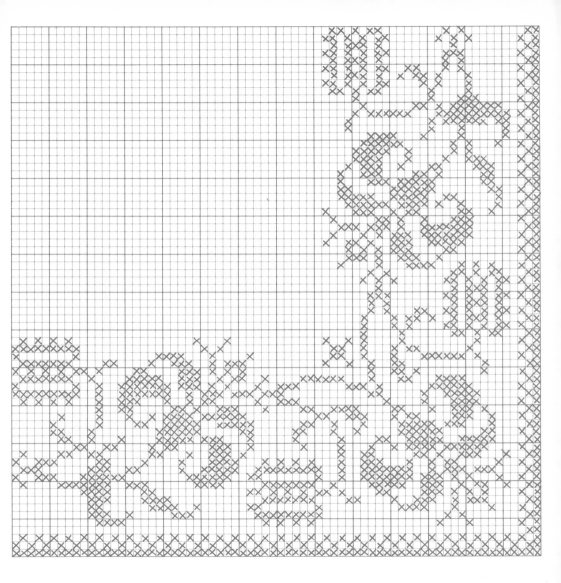

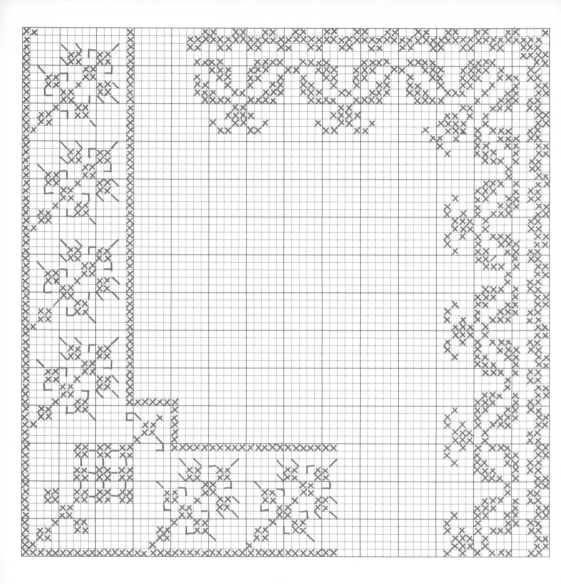

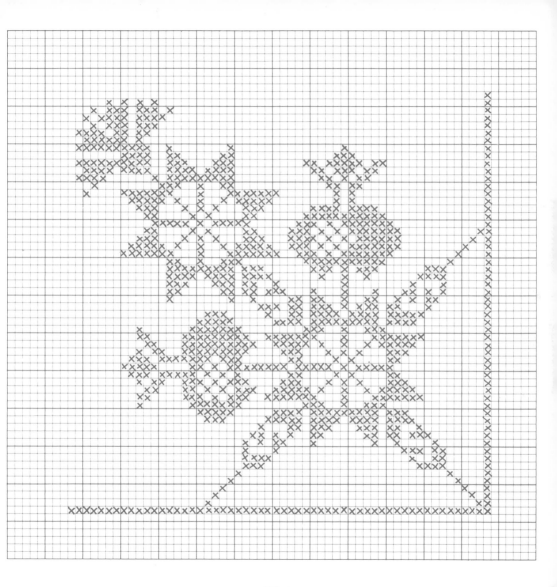

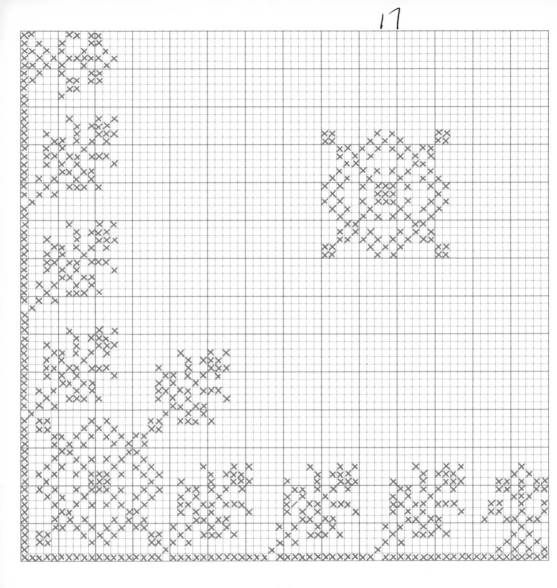

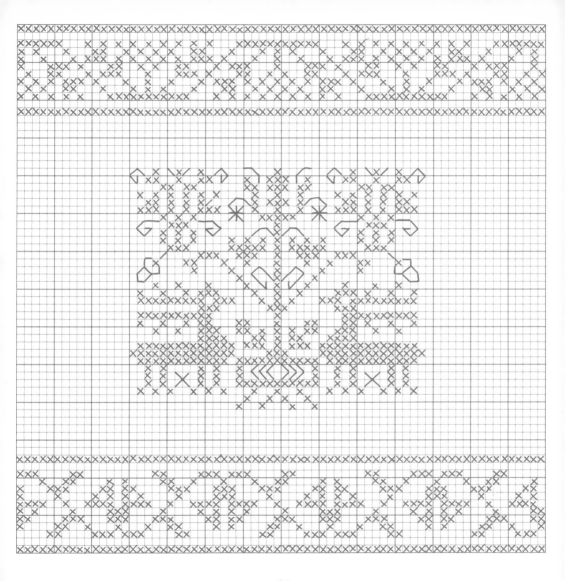

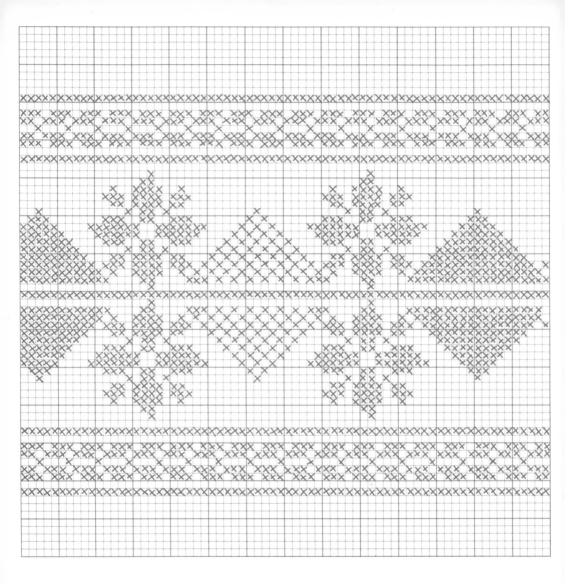

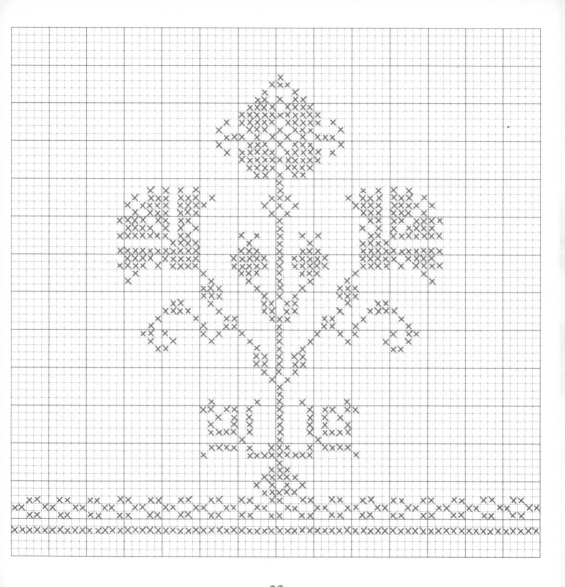

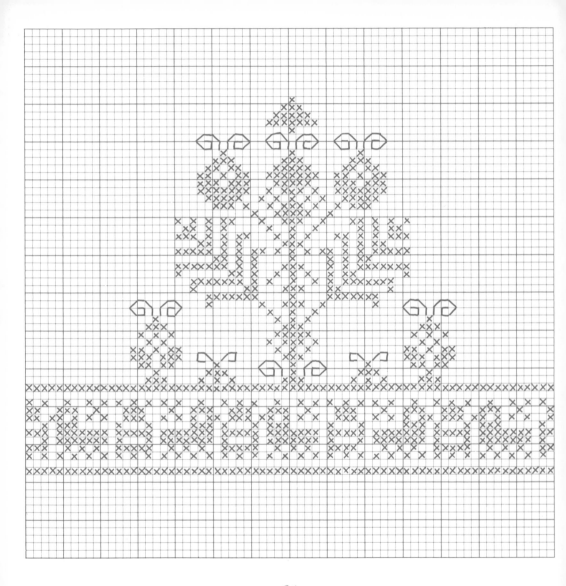

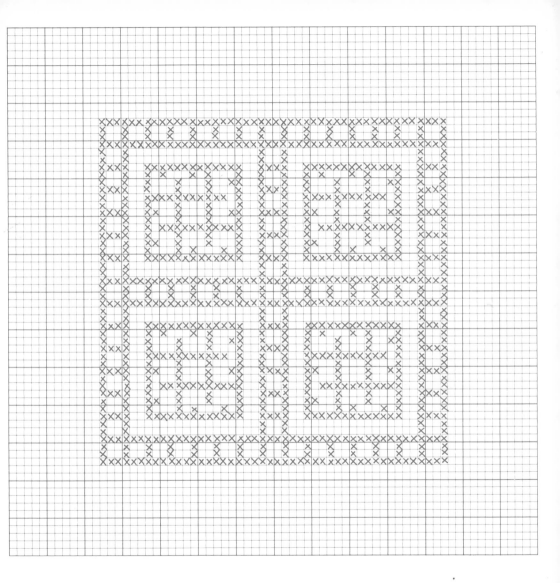

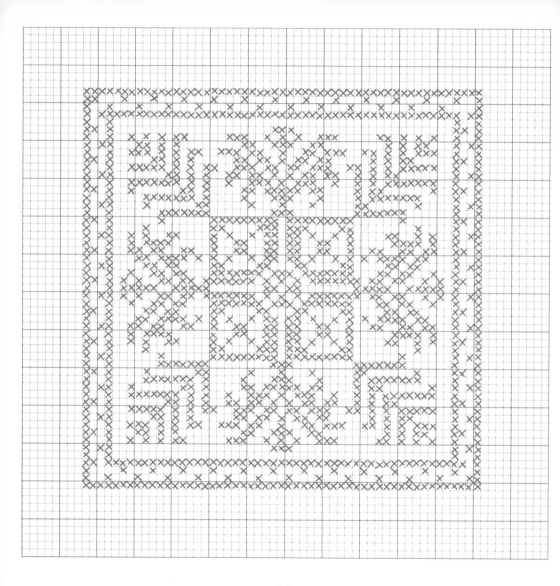

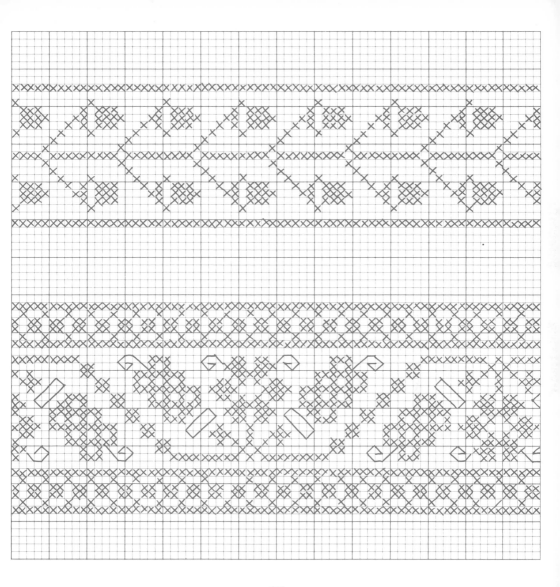

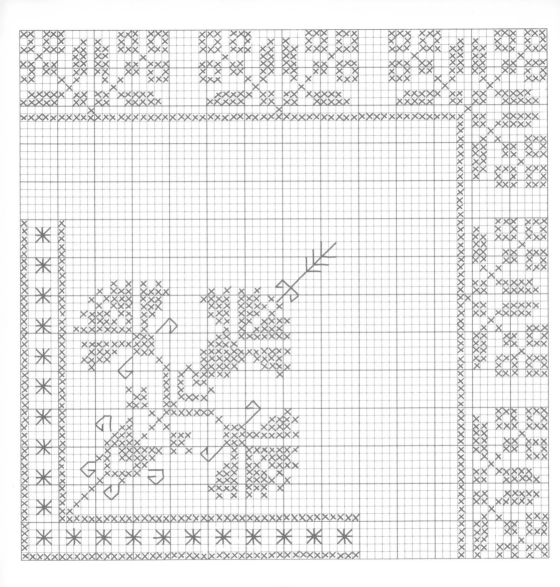

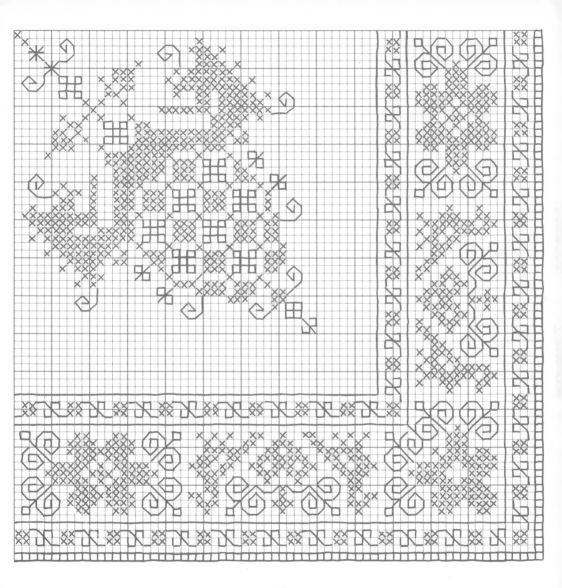

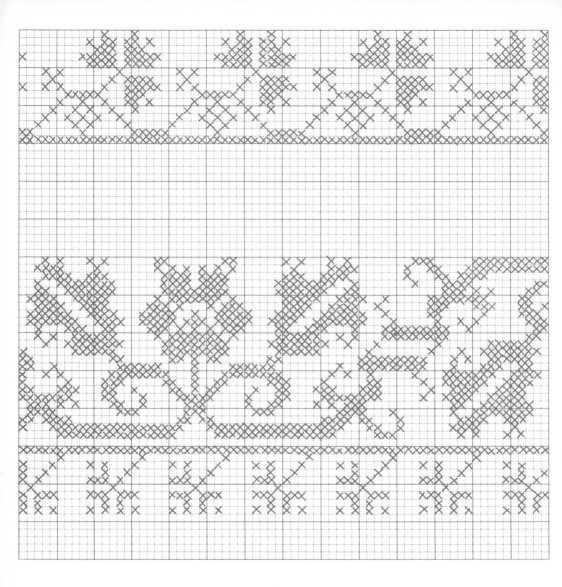

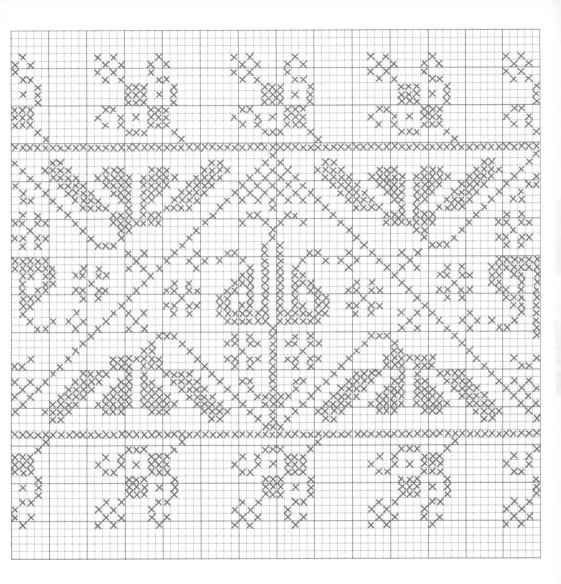

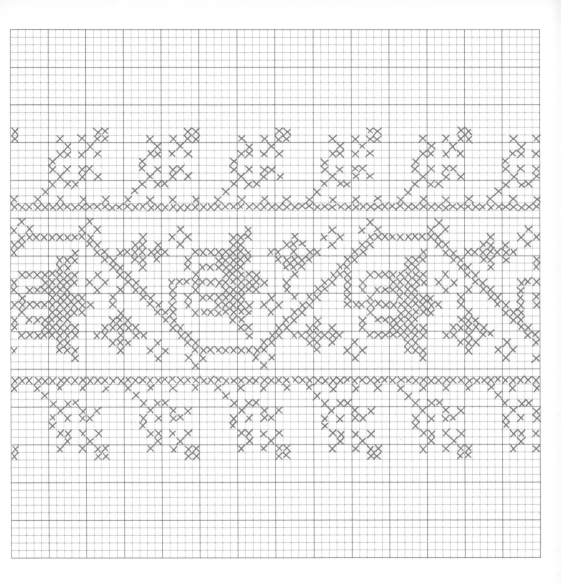

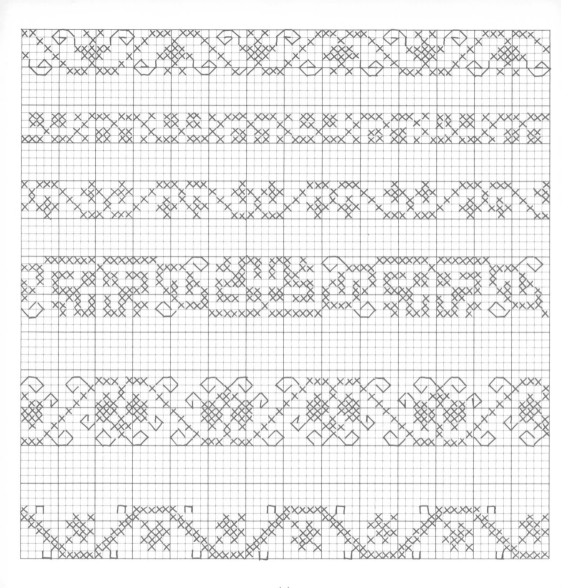

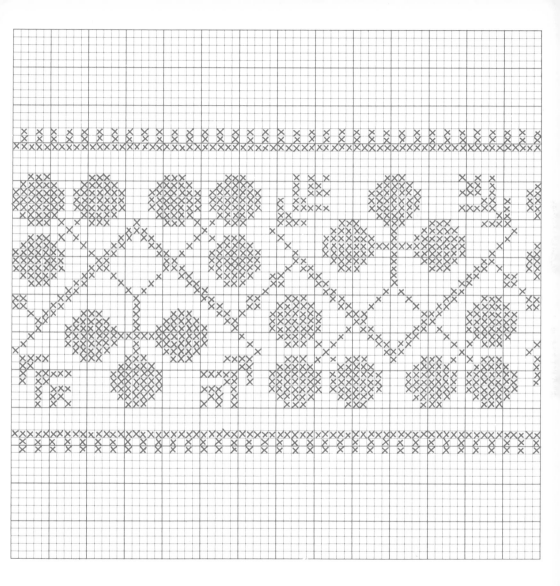

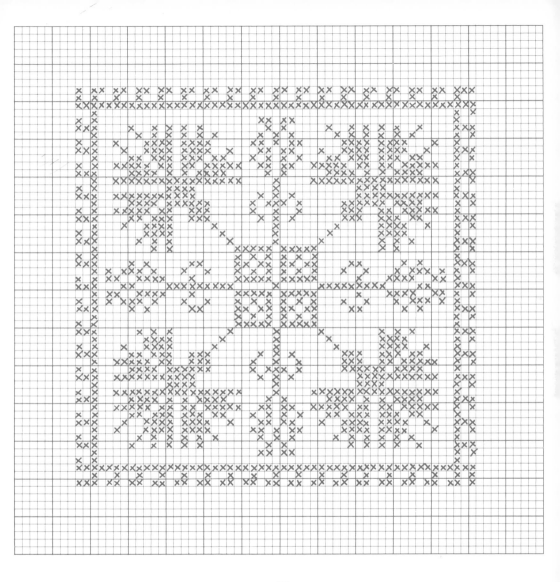

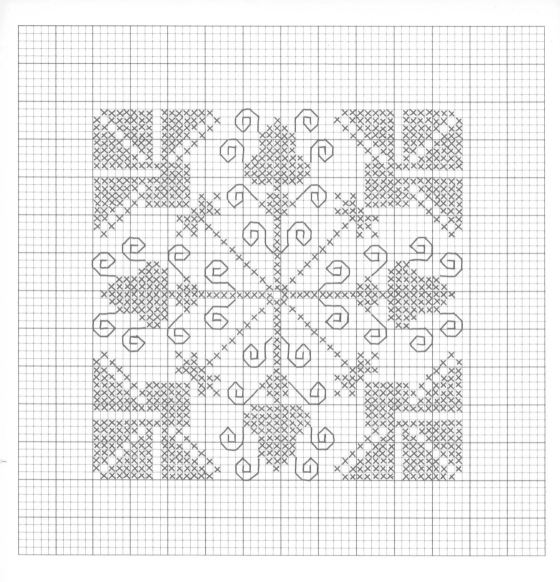

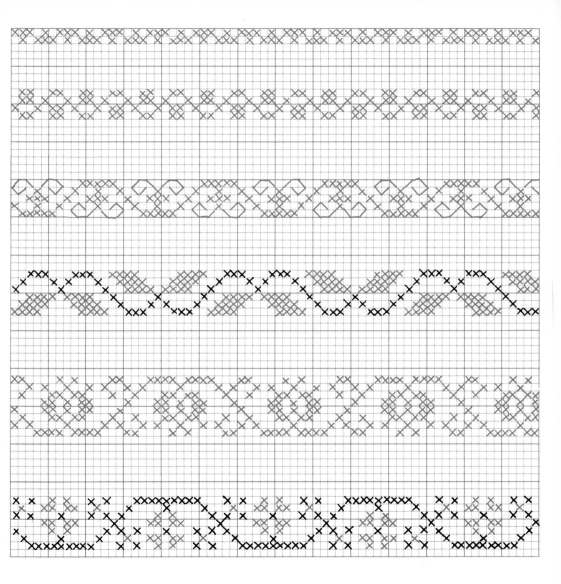

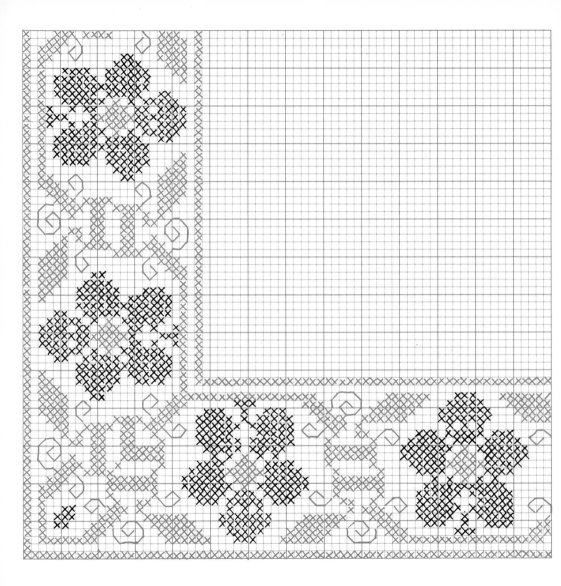

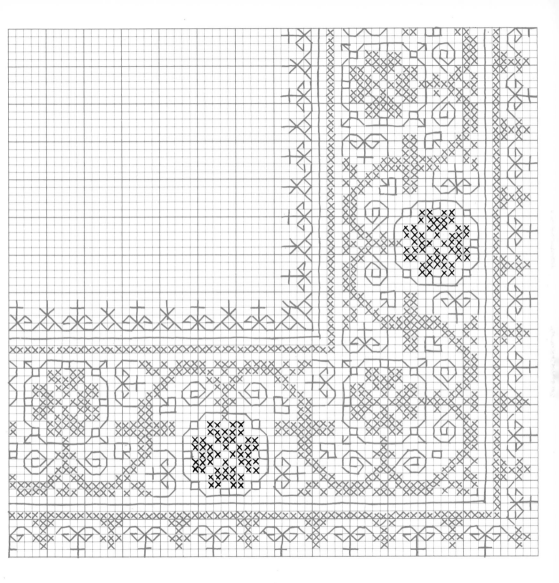

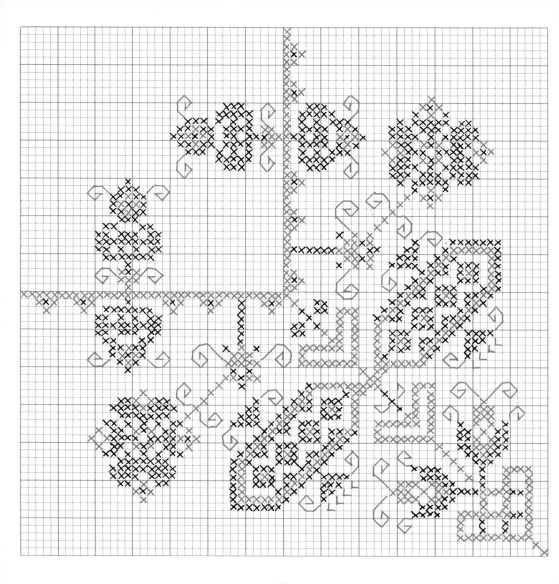

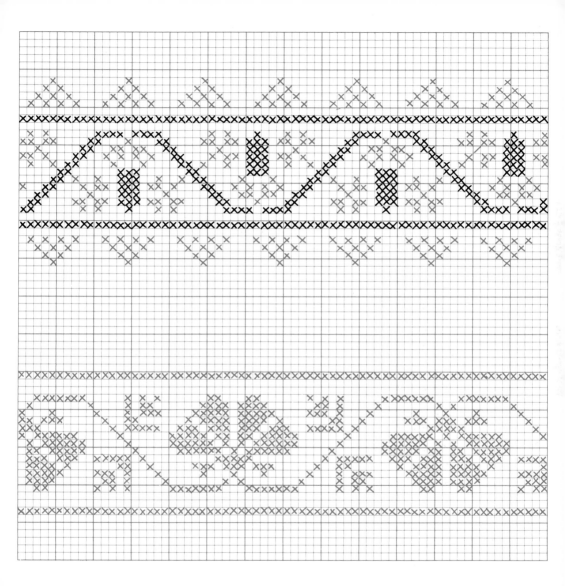

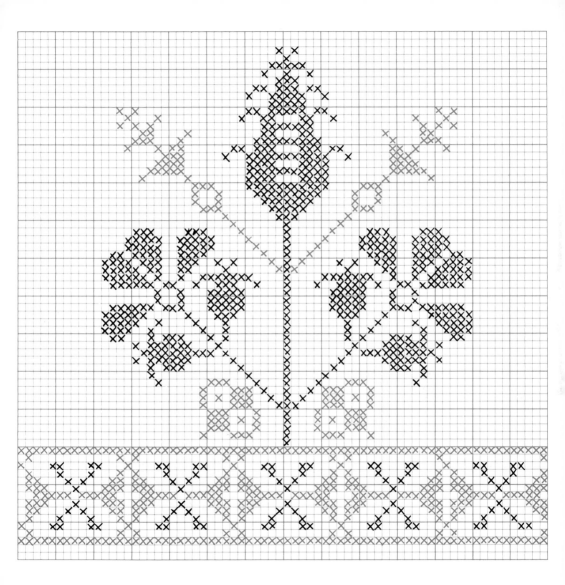

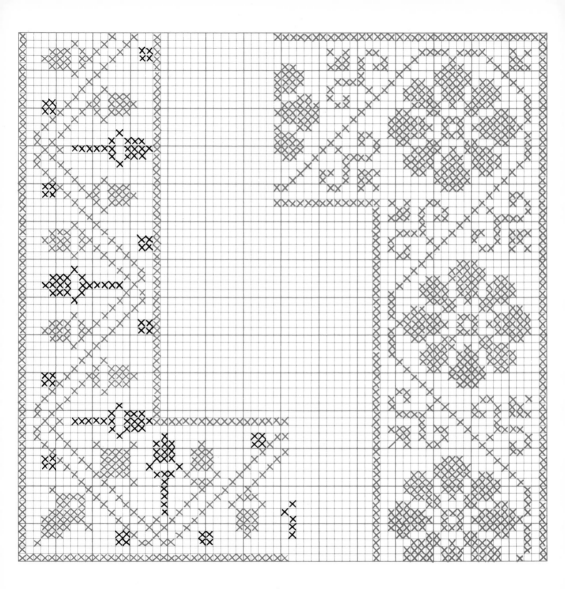

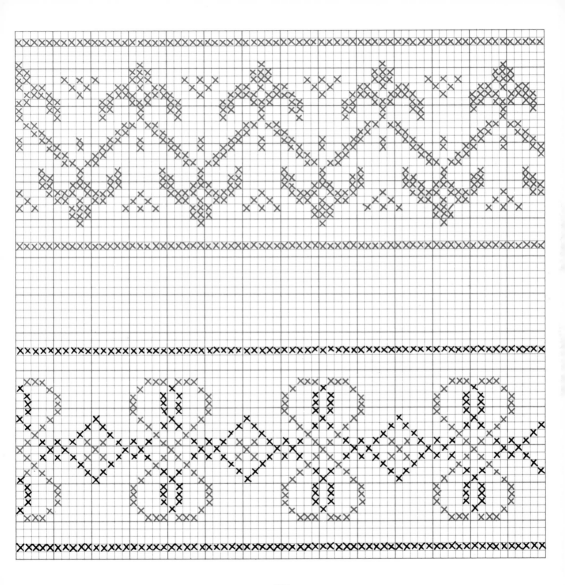

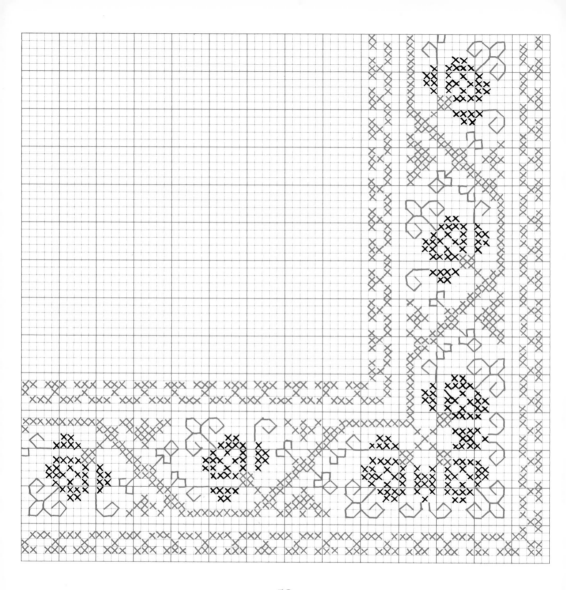

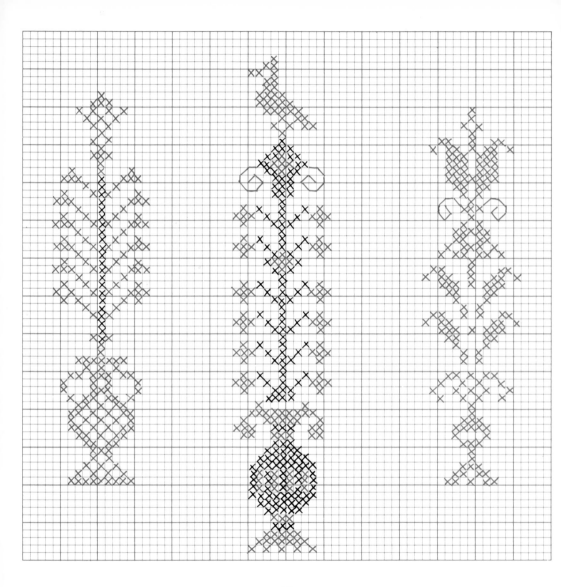

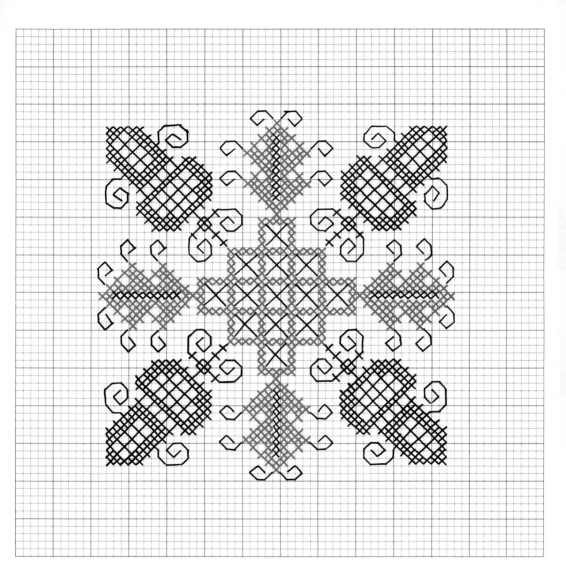

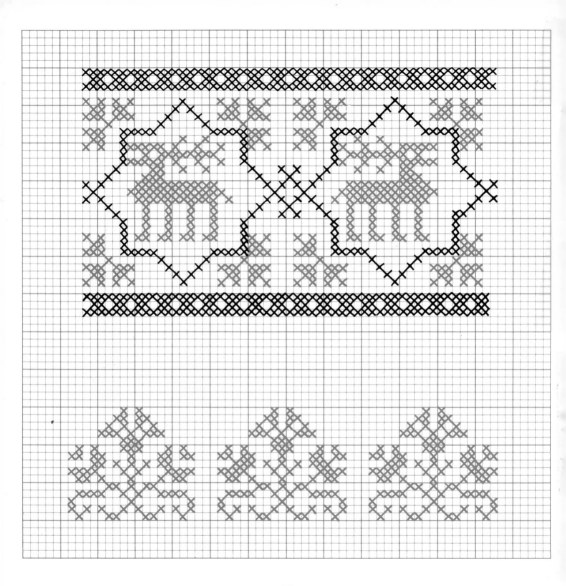

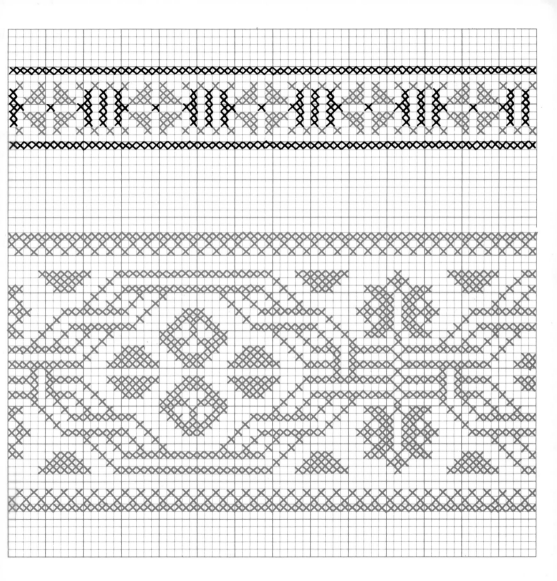

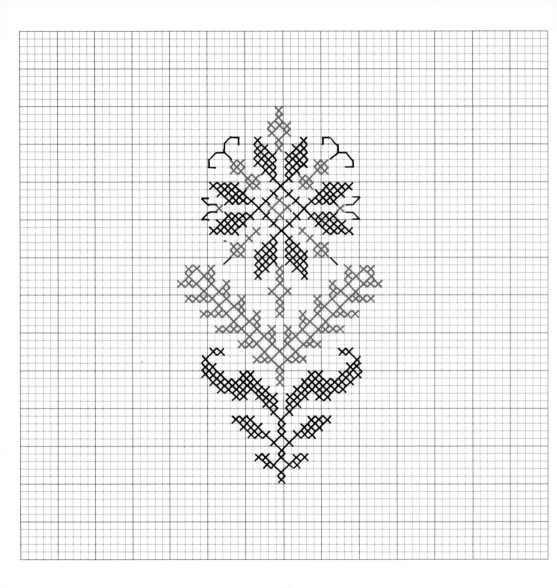

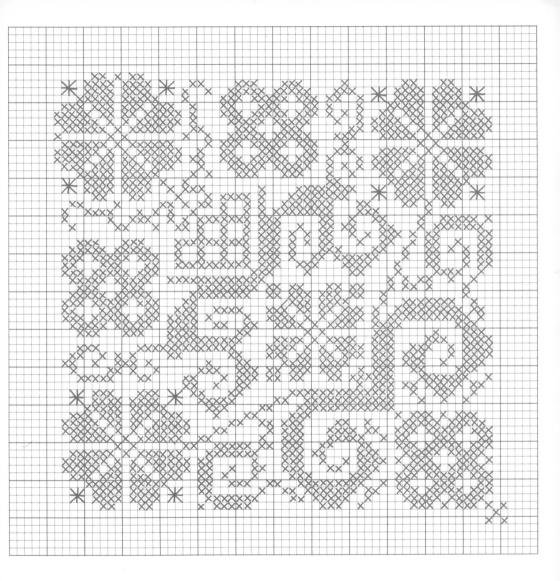

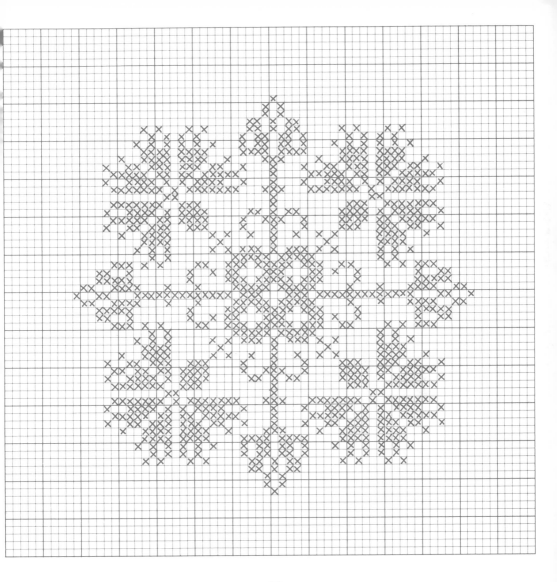

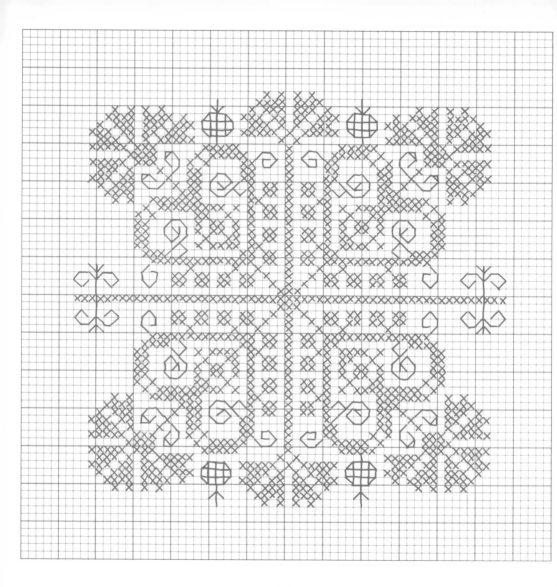

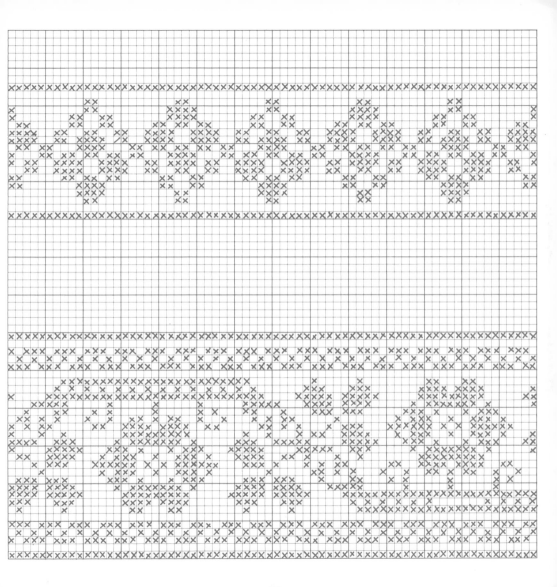

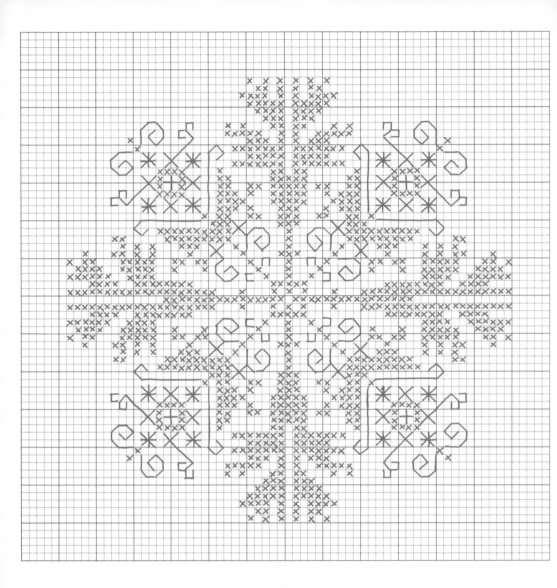

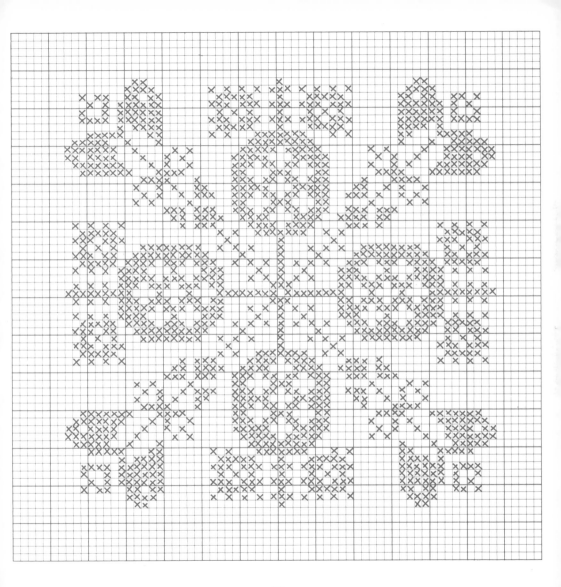

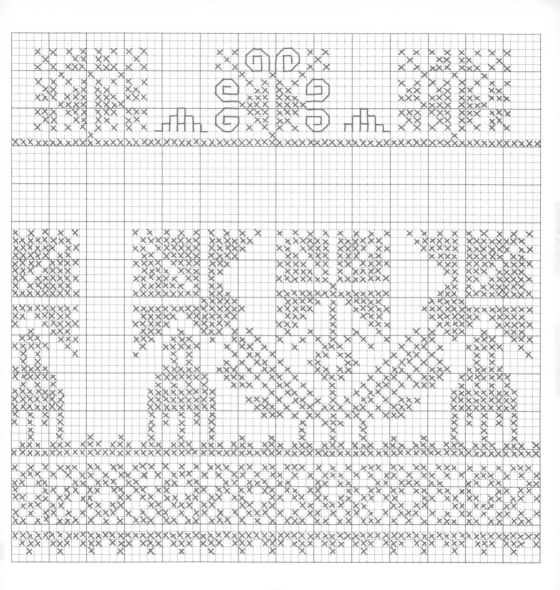

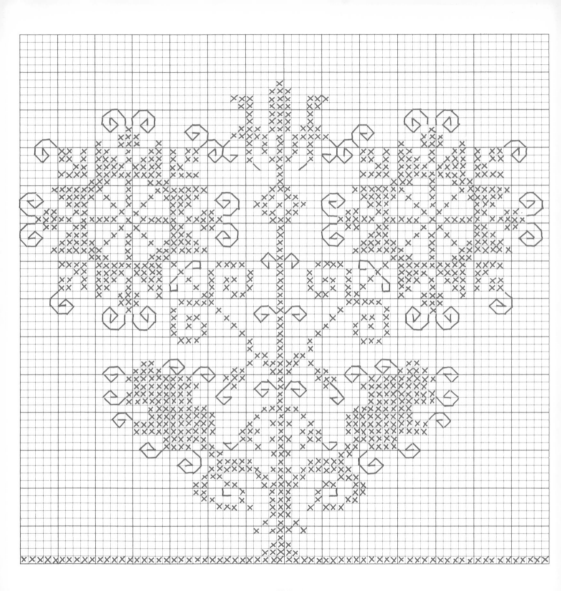

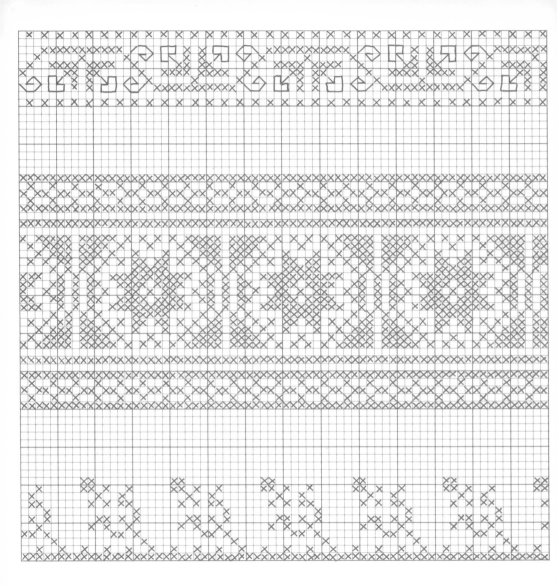

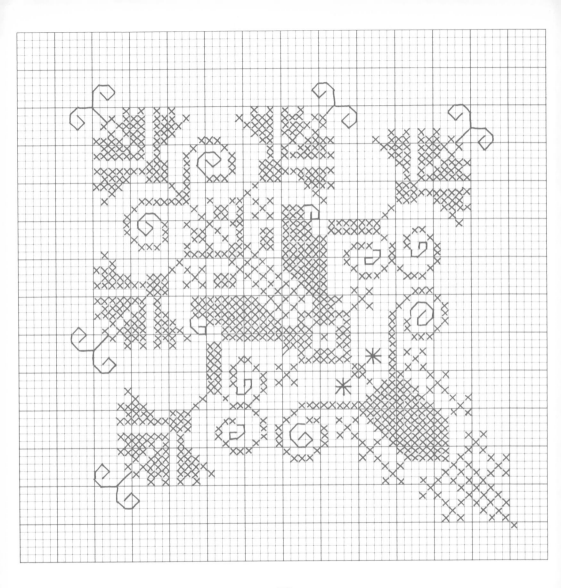

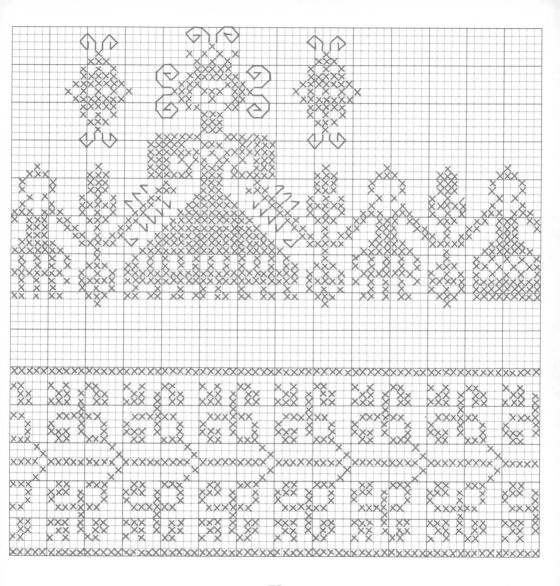

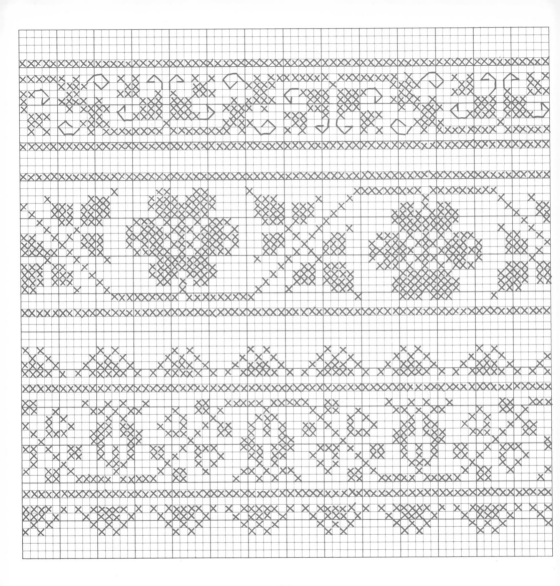

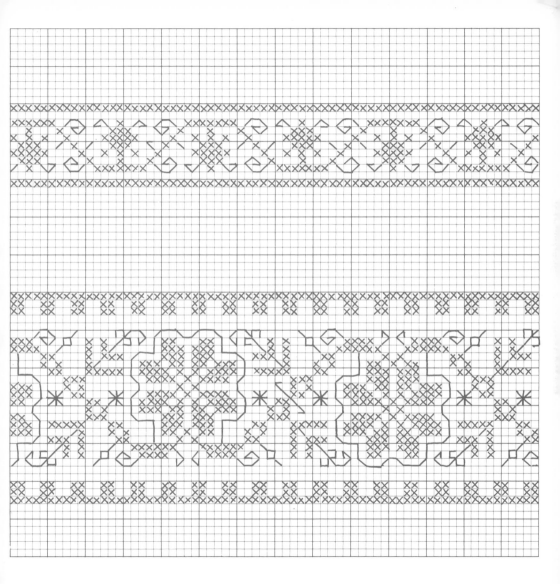

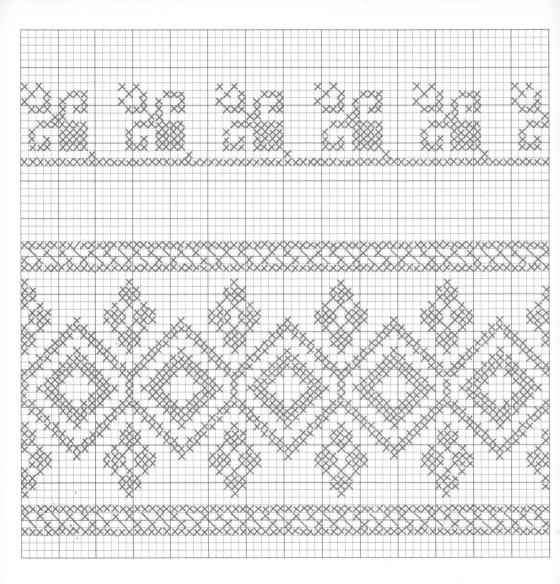

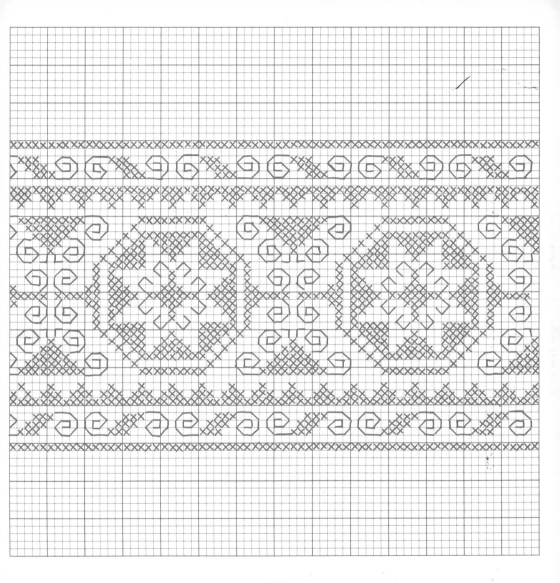

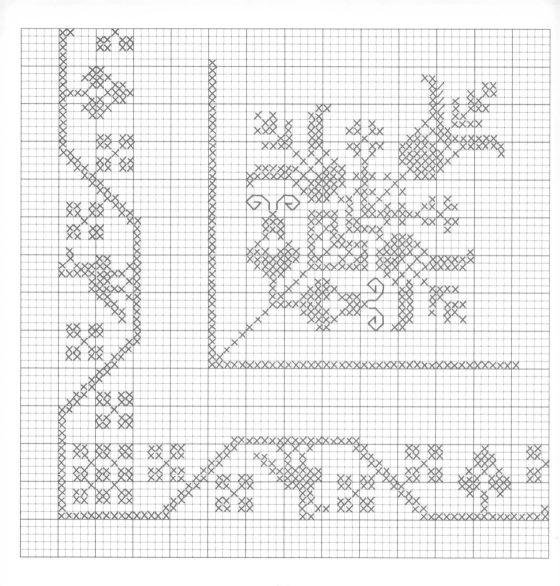

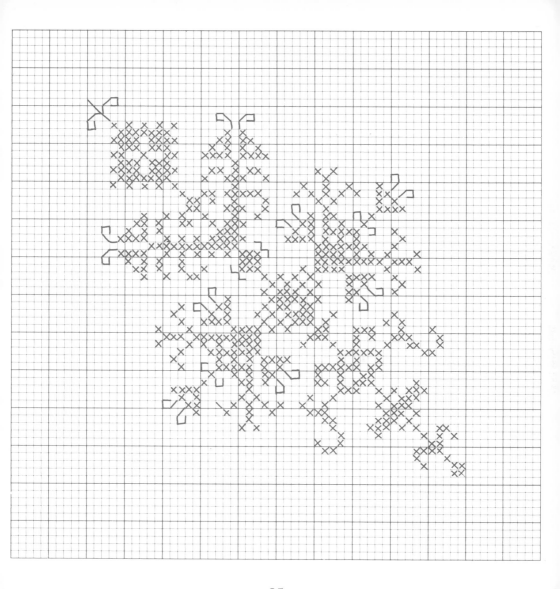

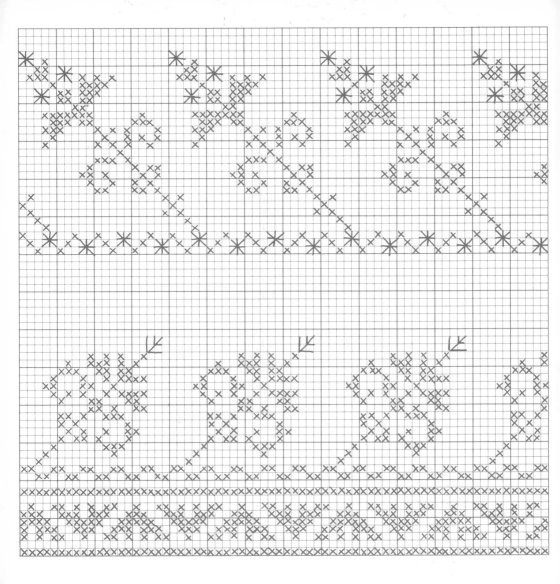

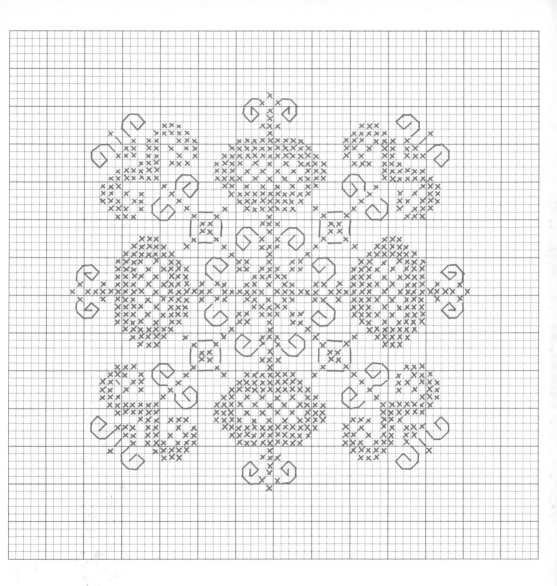

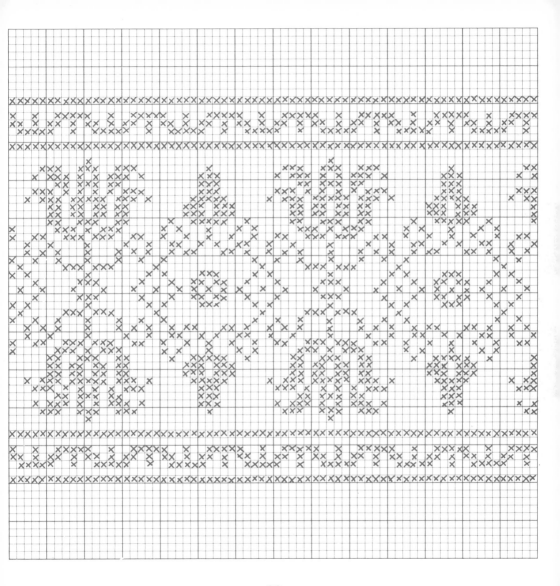

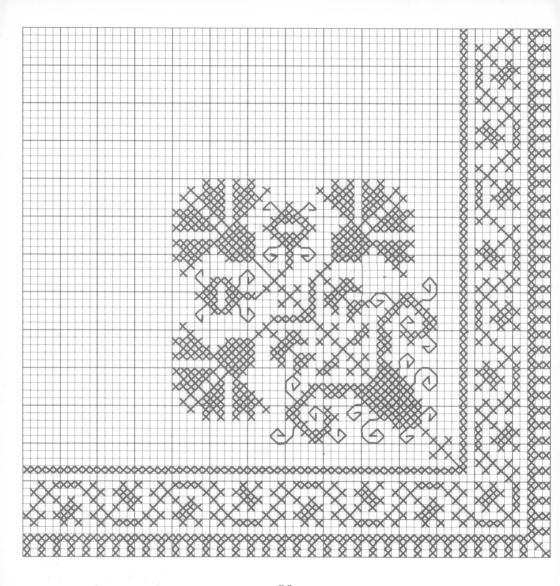

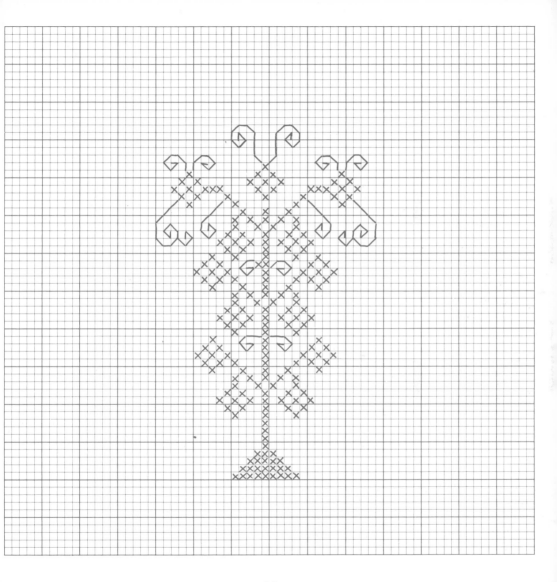

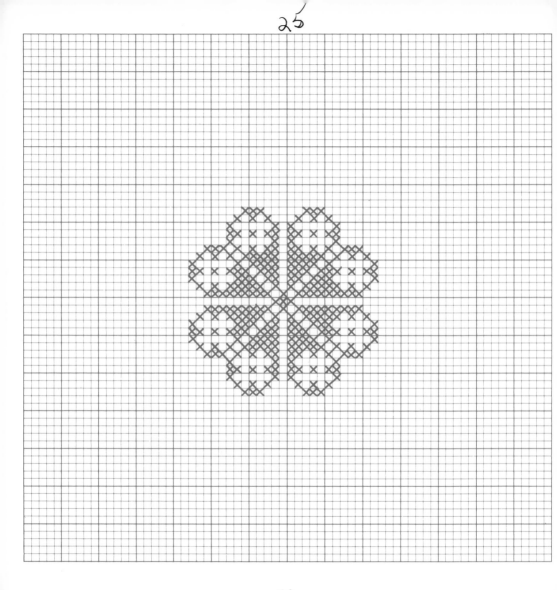

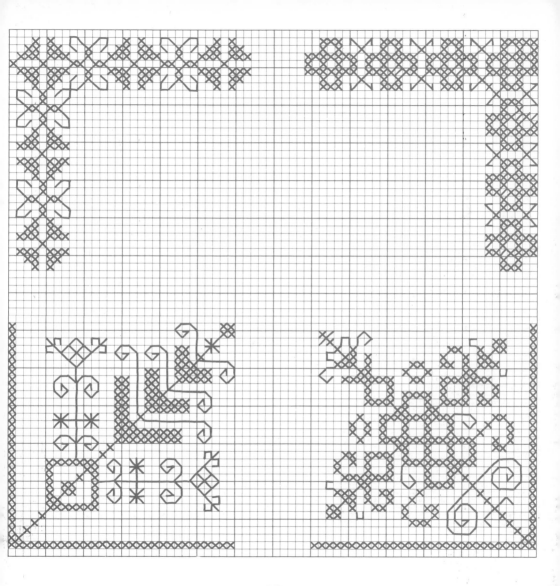

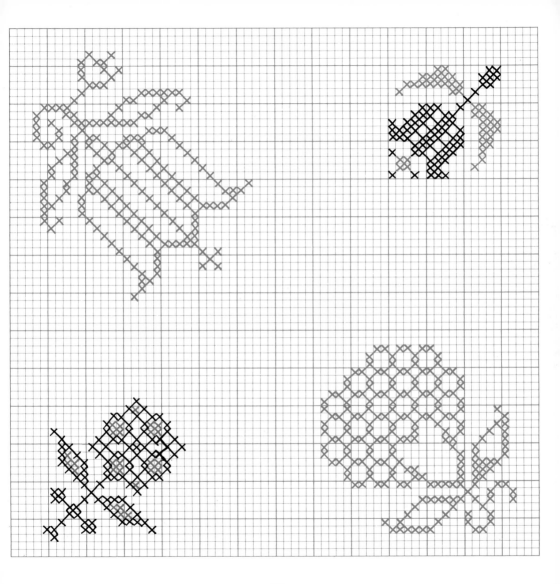

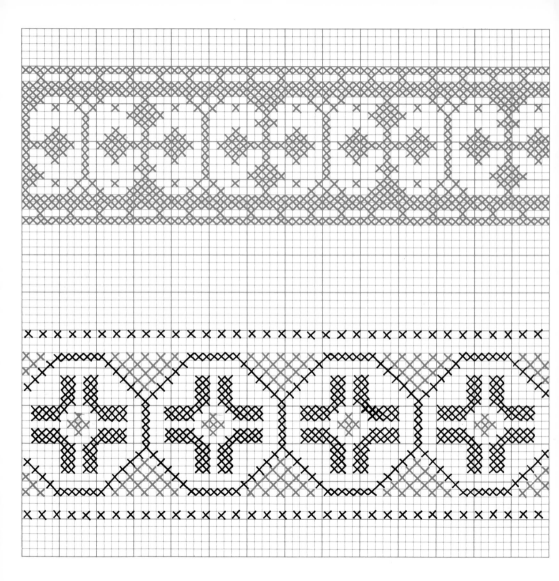

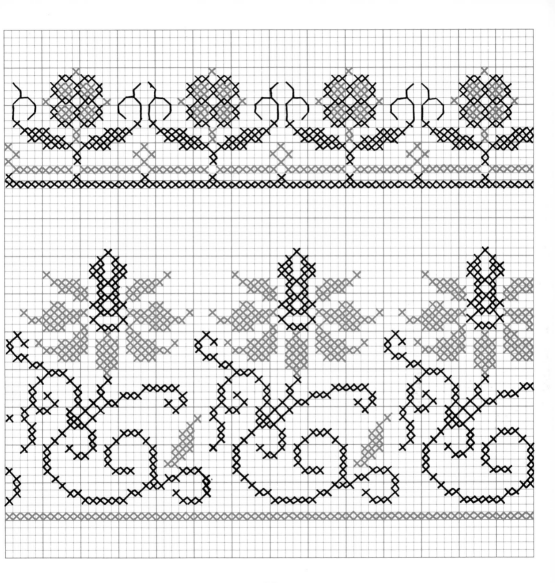

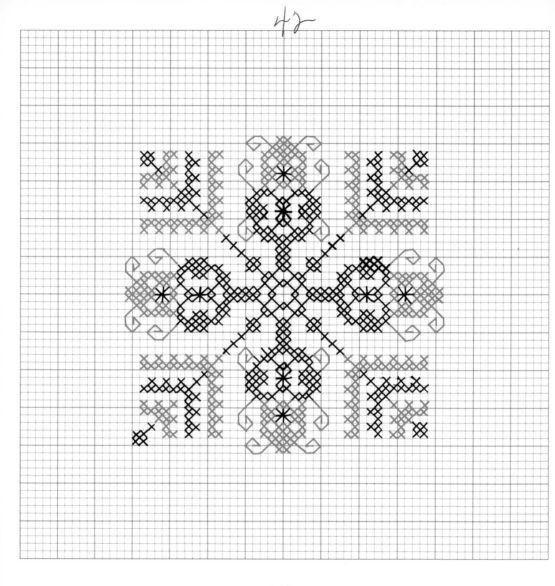

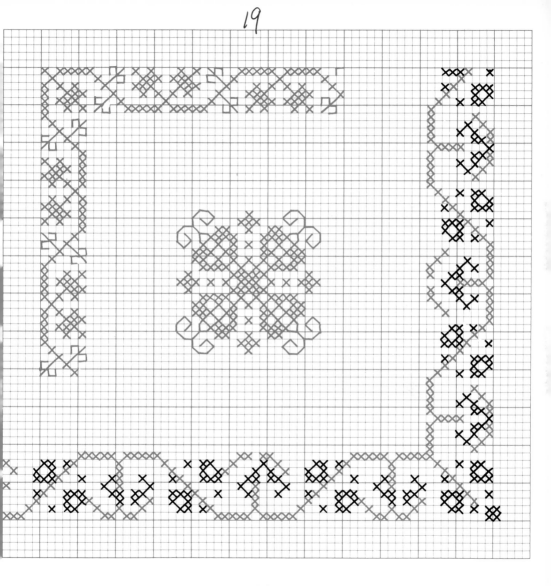

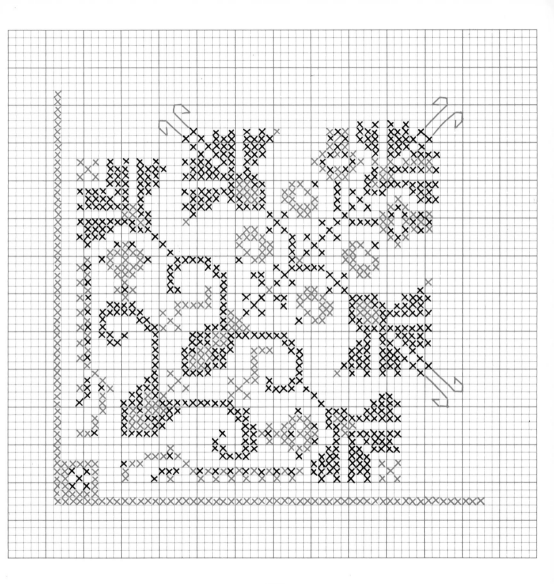

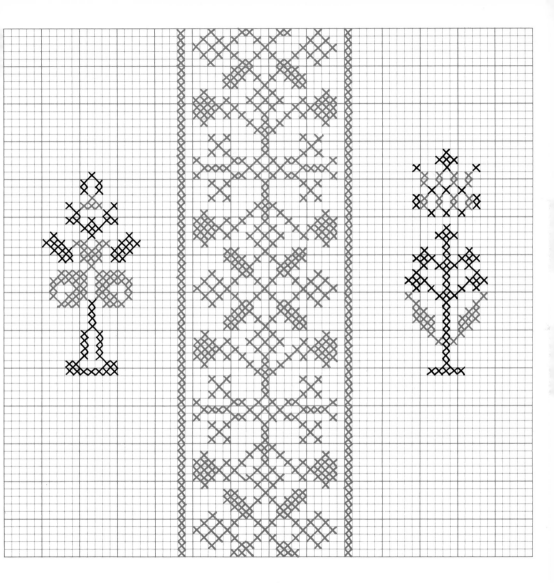

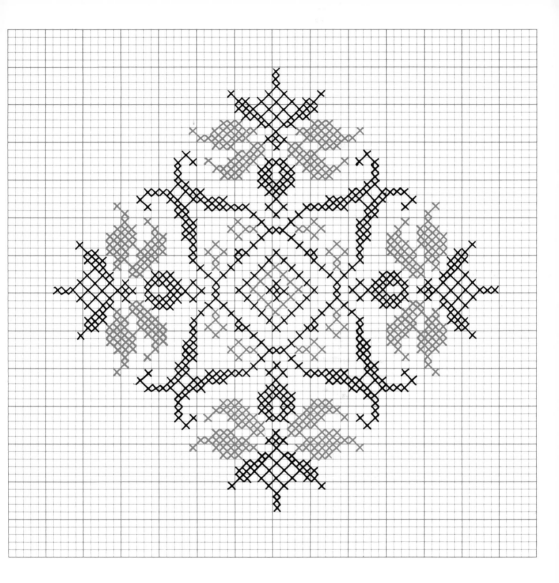

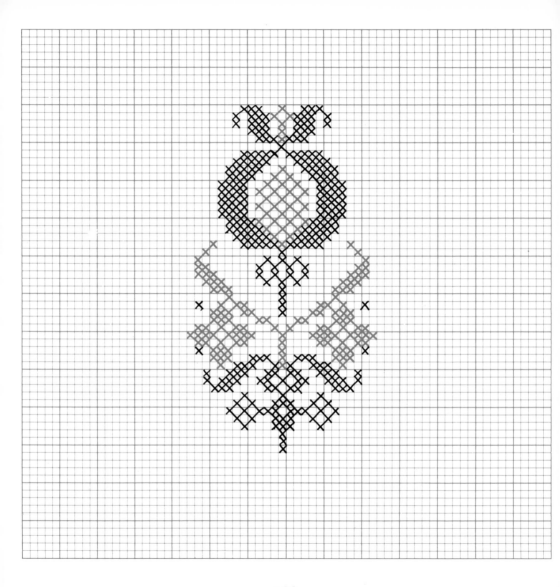

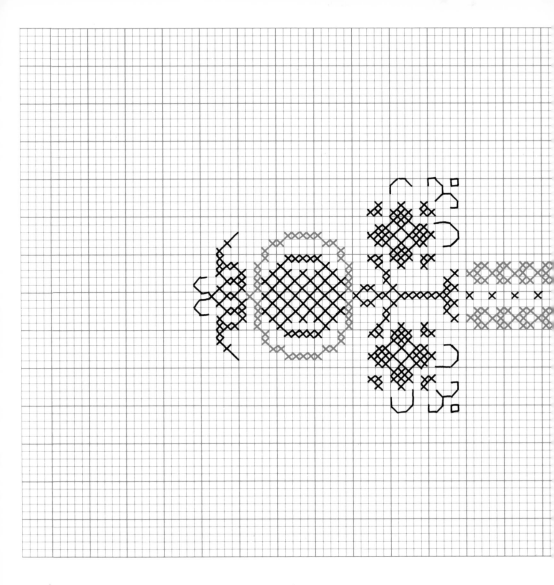

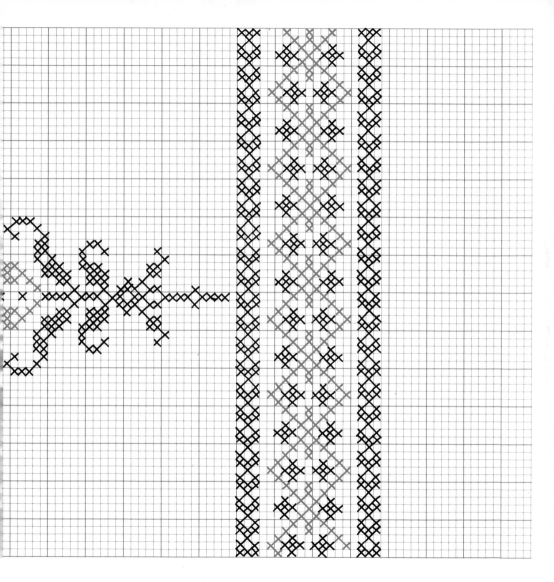

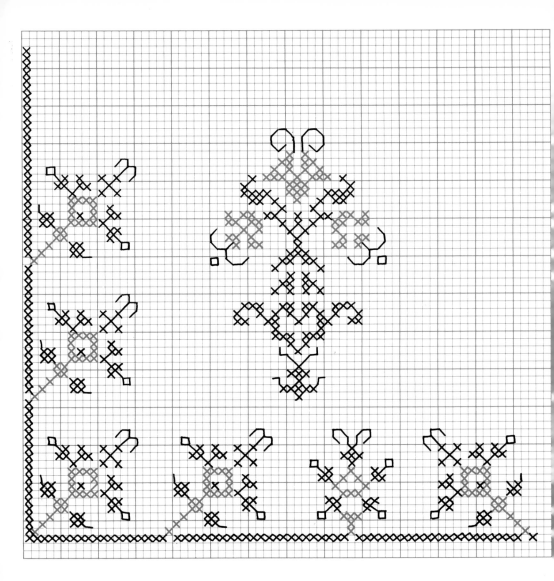

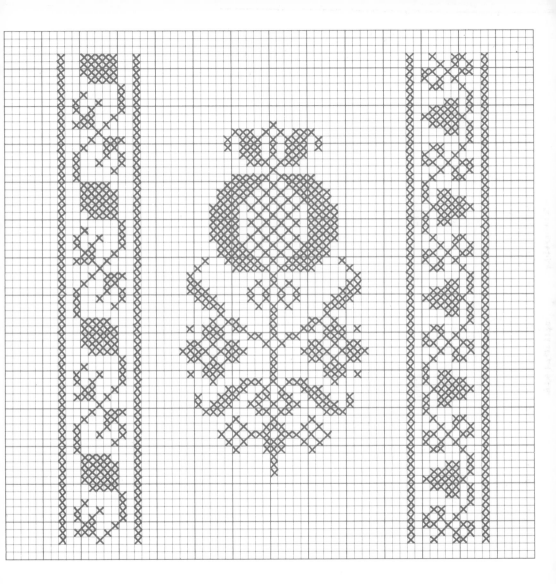

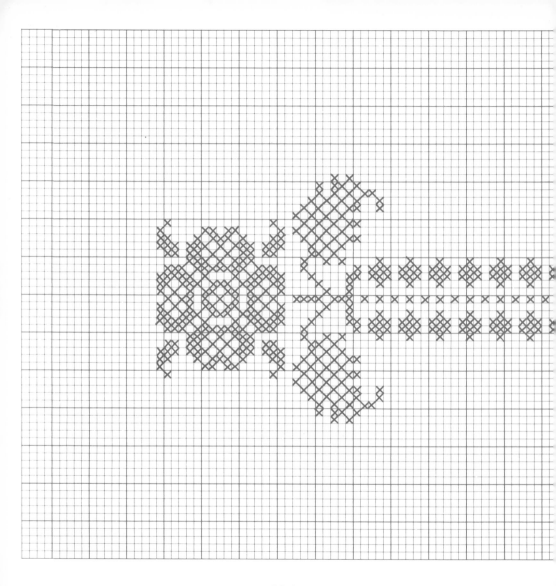

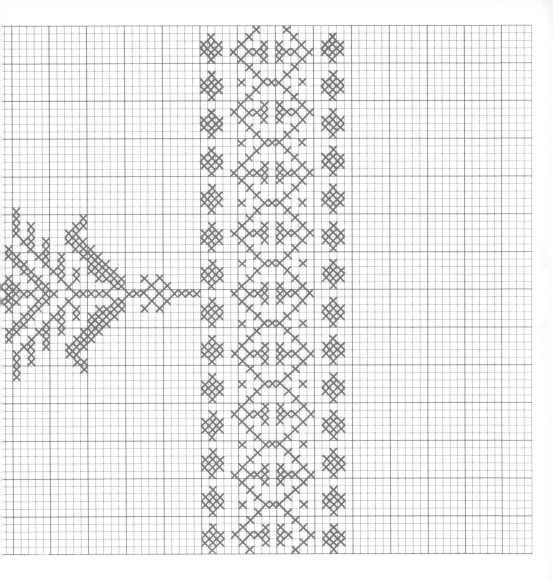

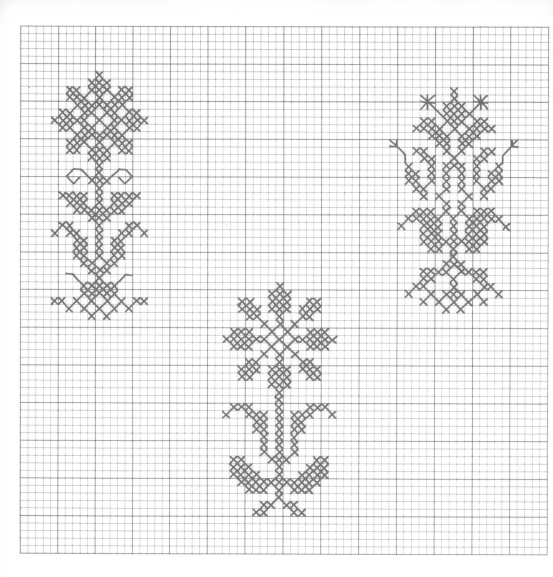

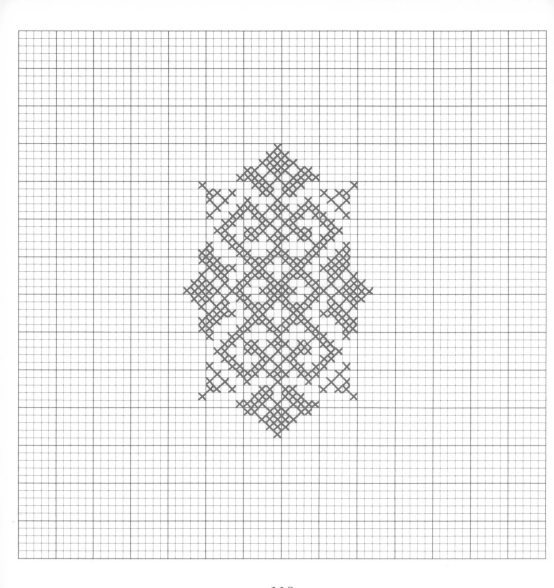

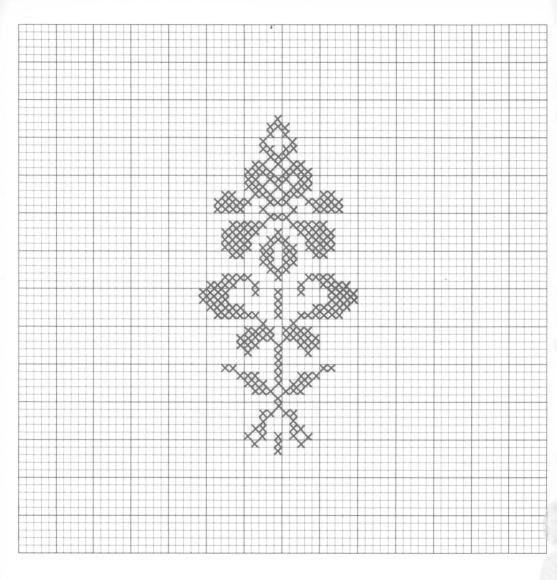

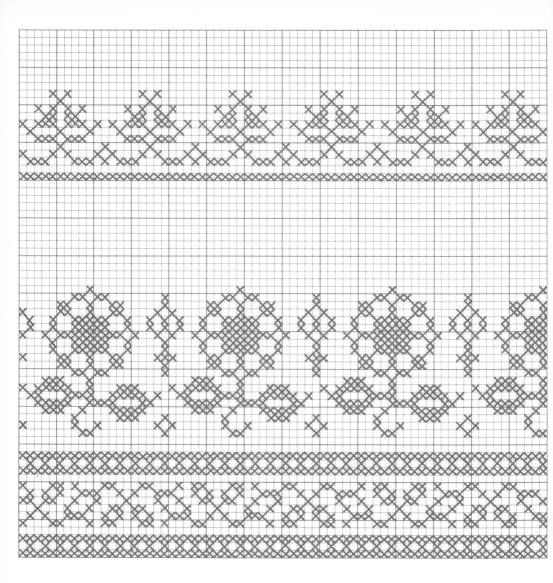

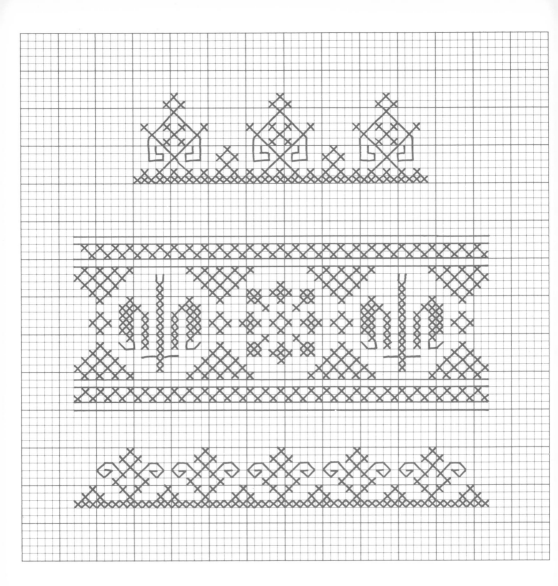

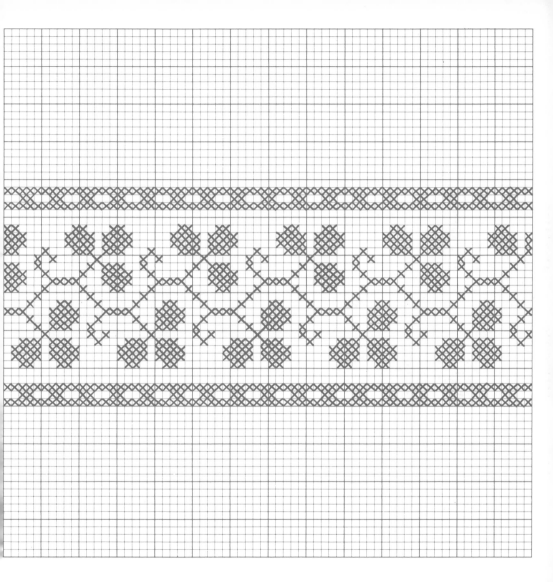

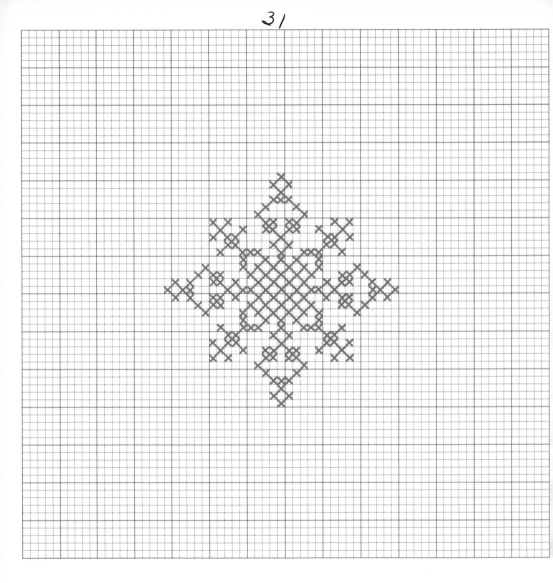

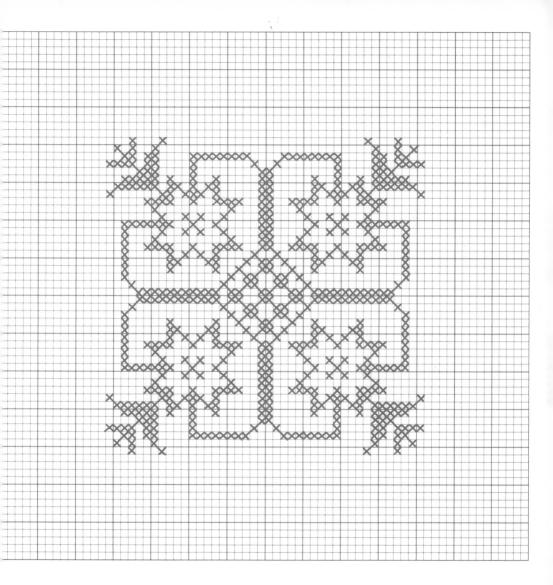

37

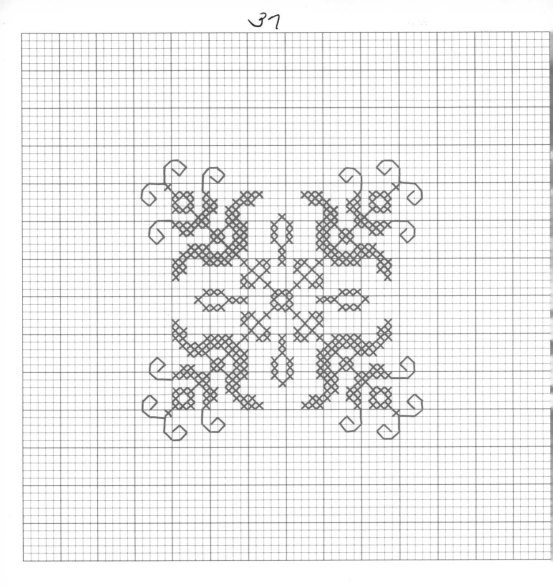

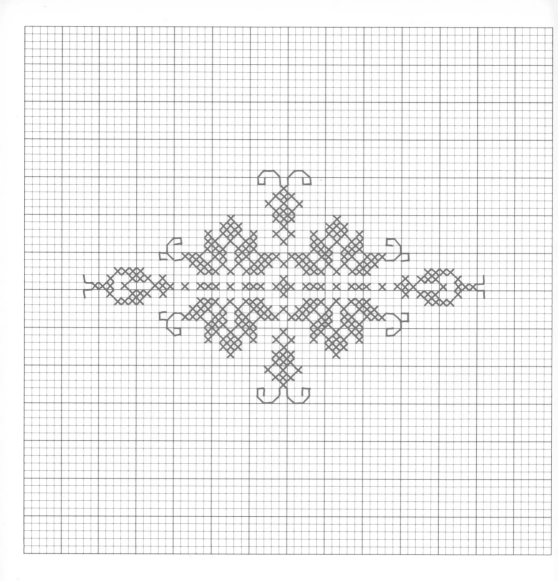

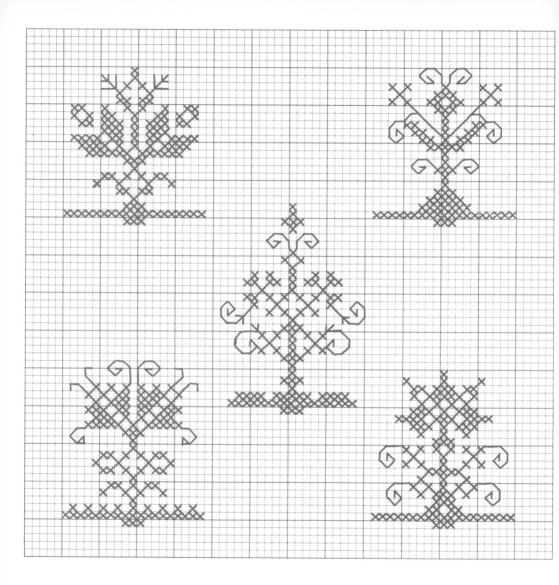

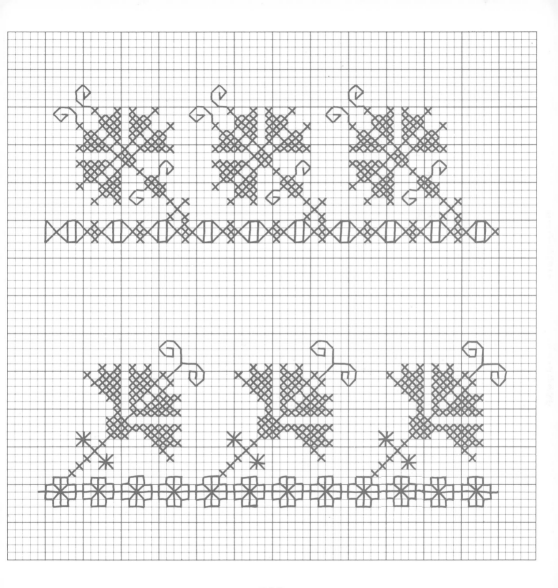

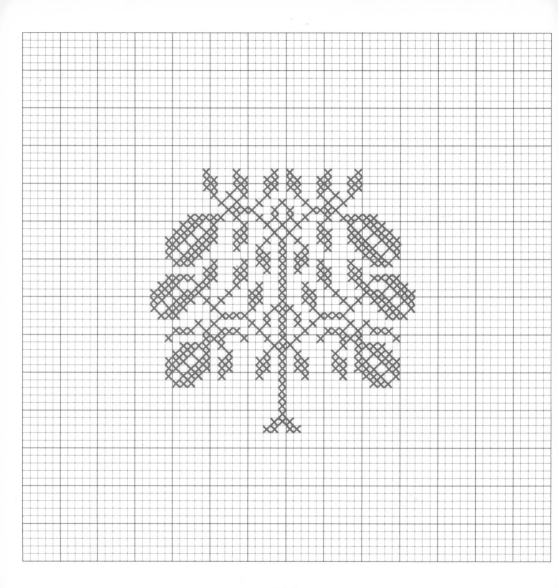

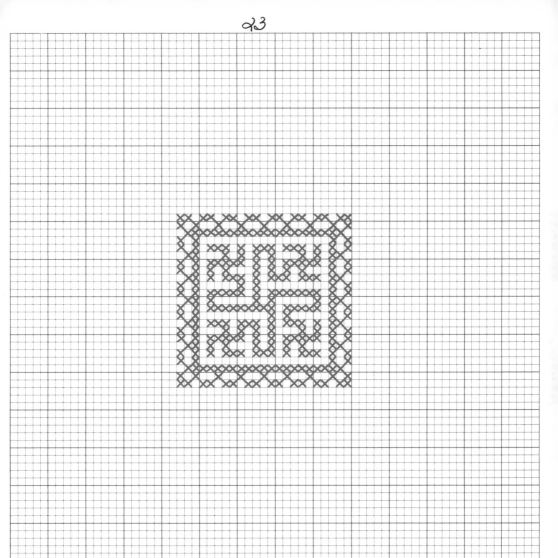

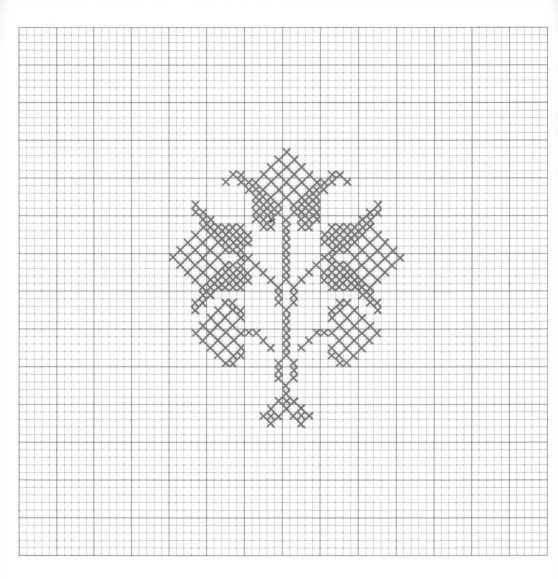

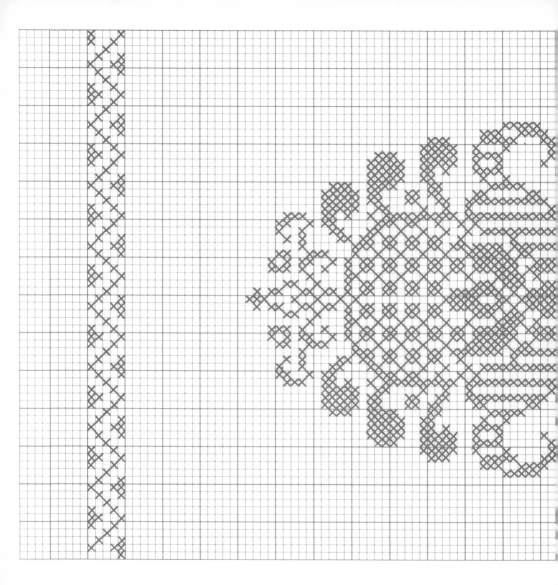

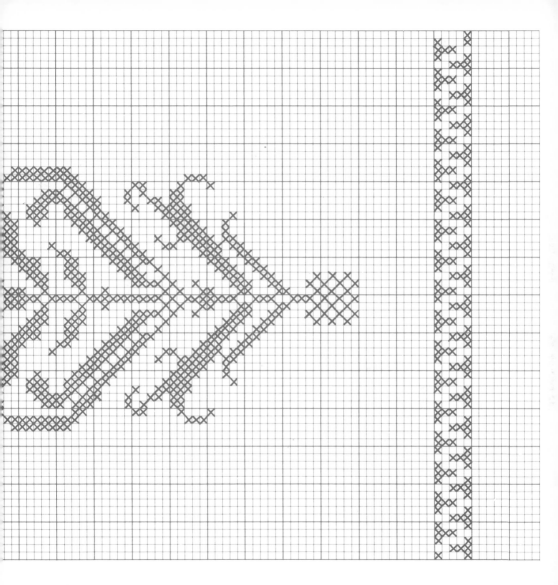

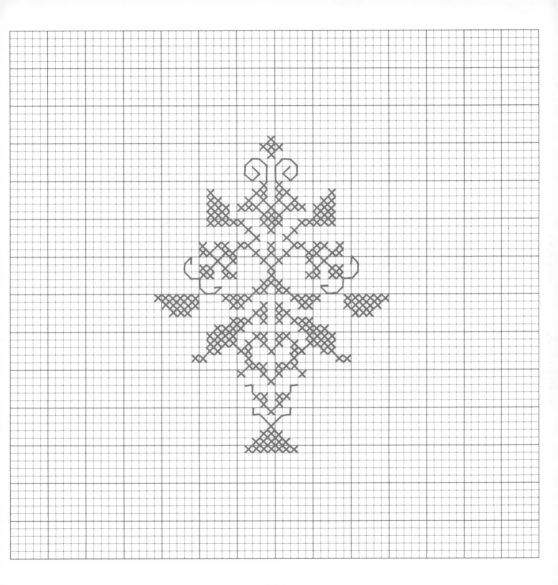

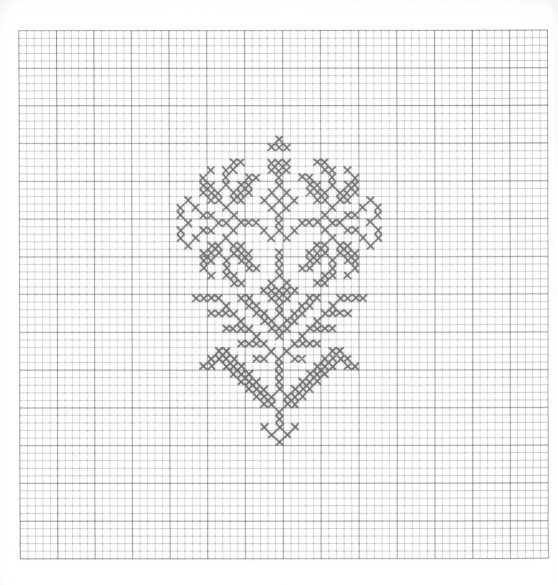

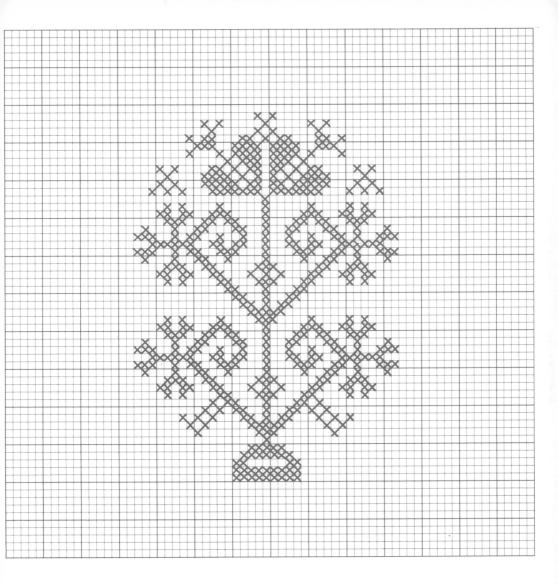

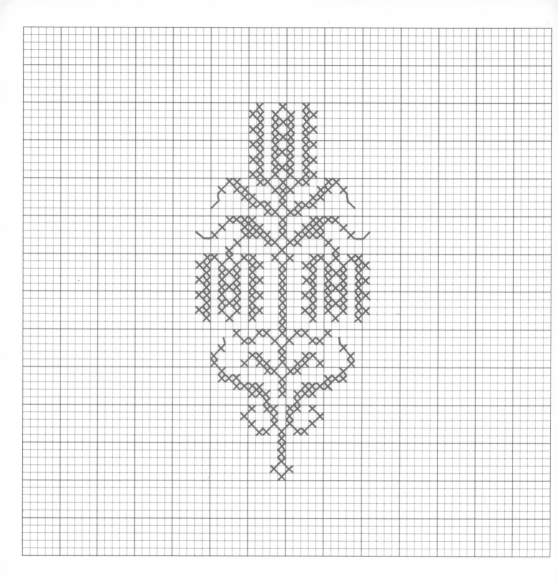

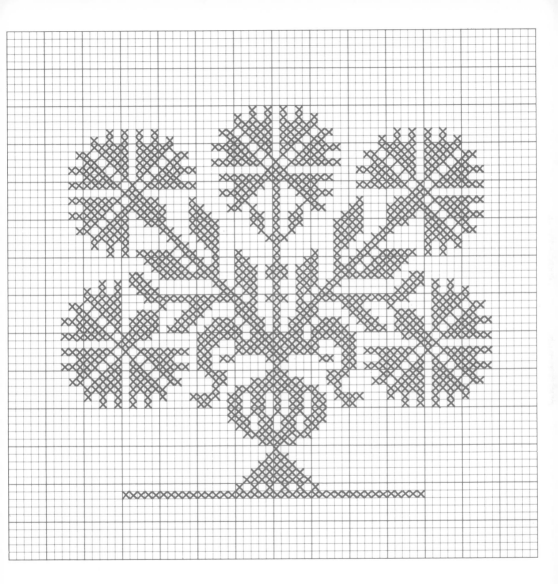

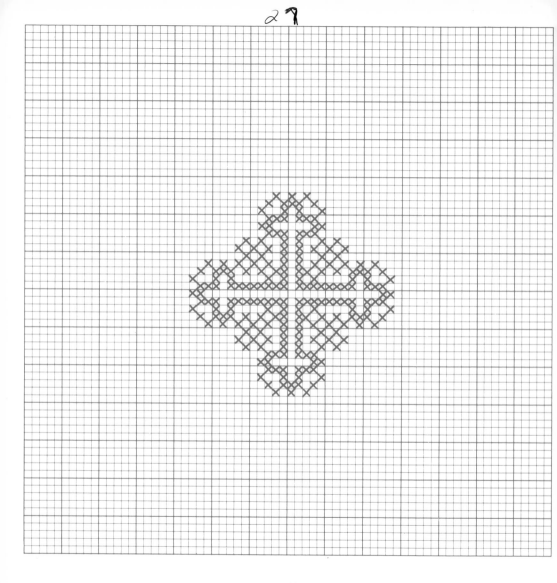

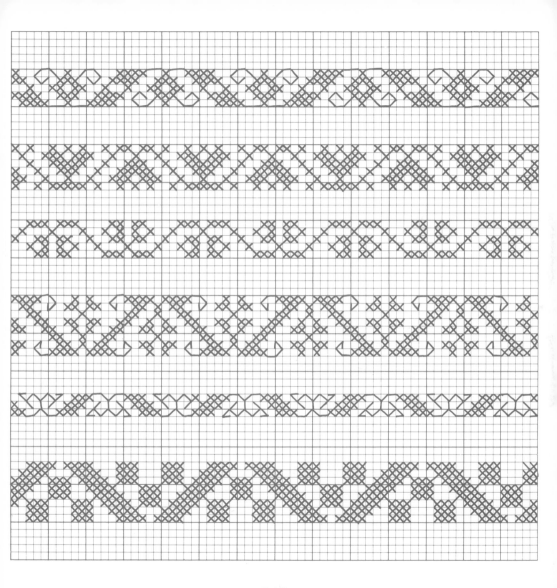

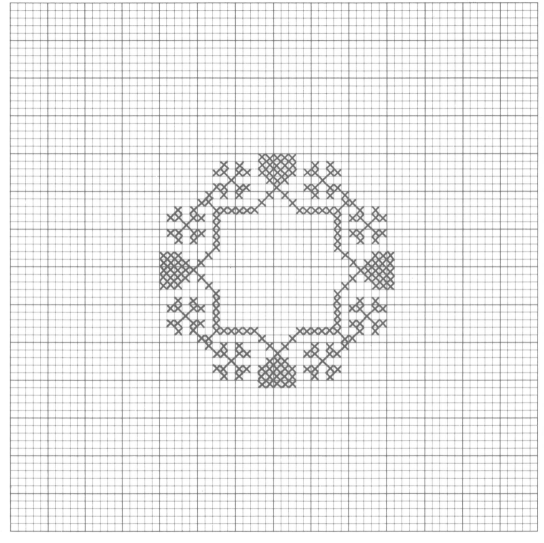

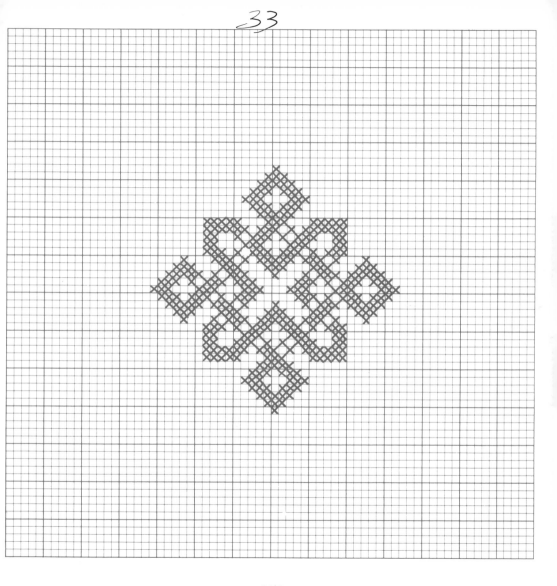

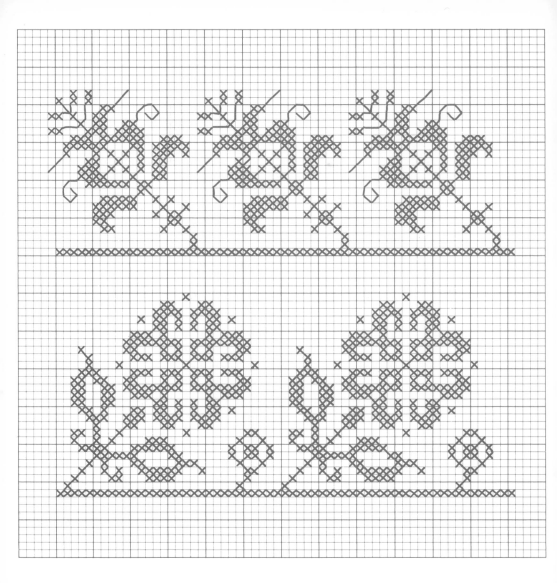

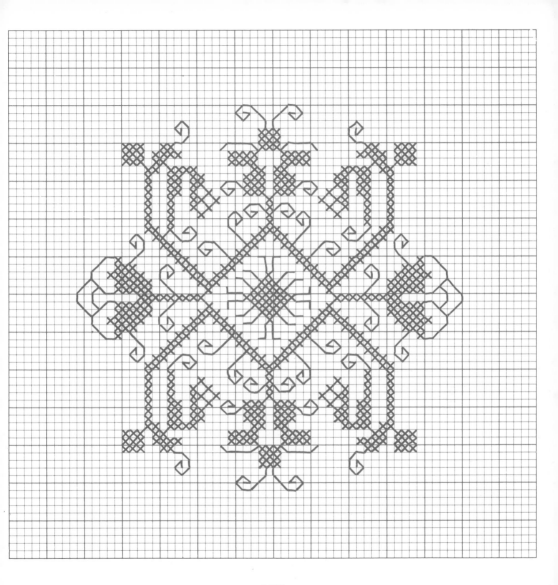

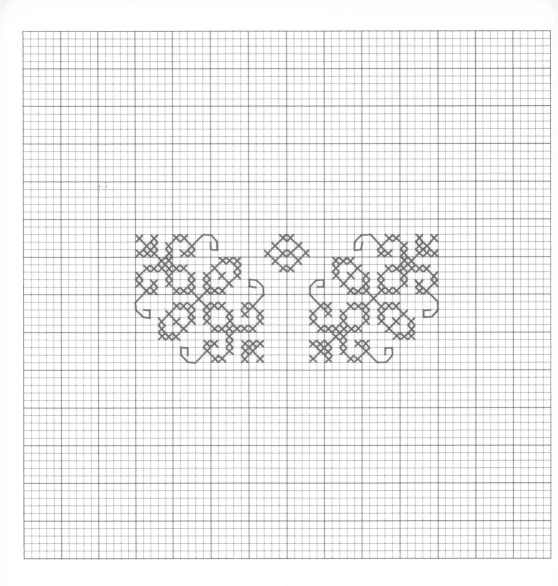

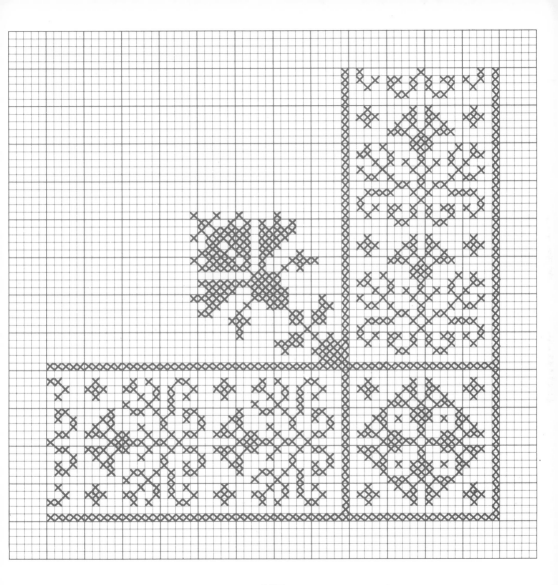

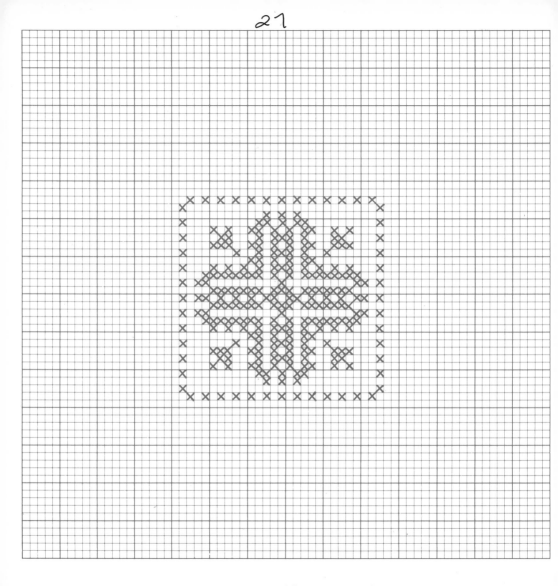

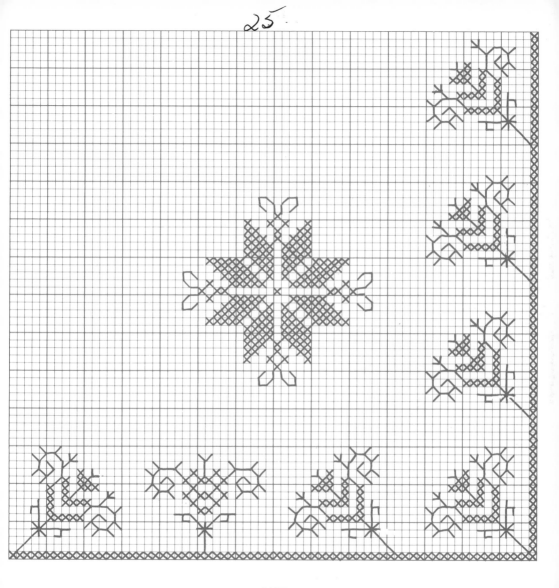

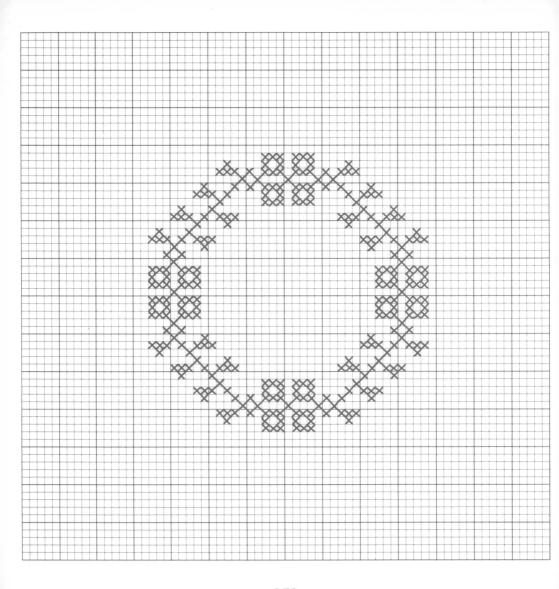

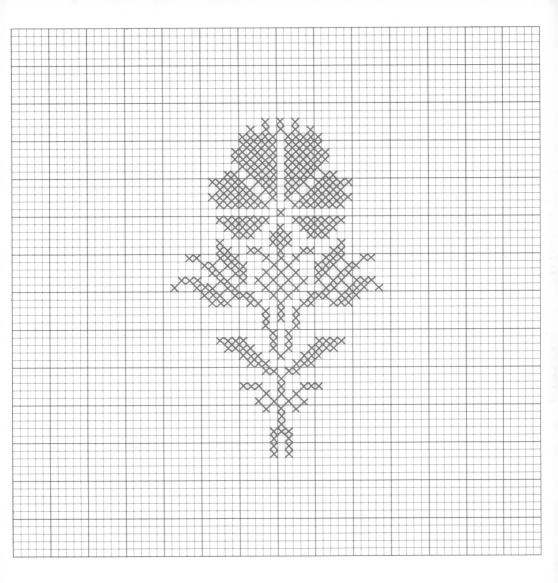

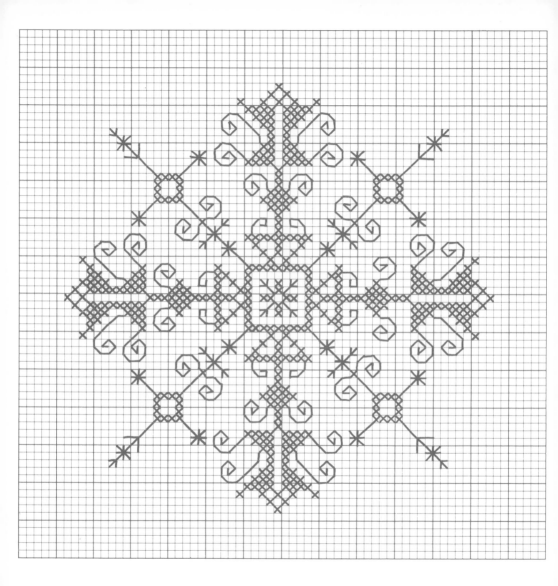

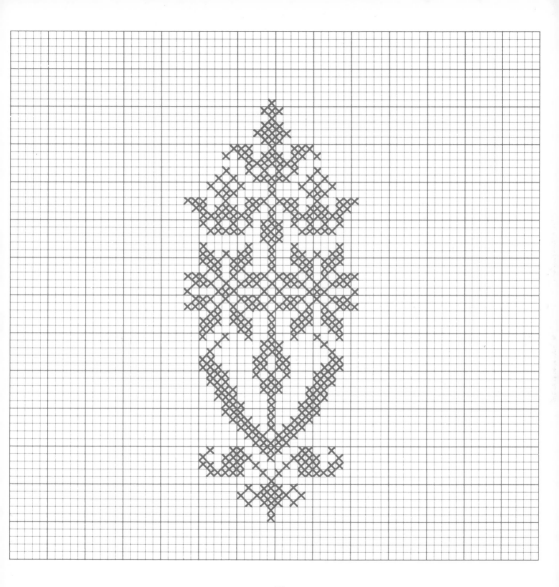

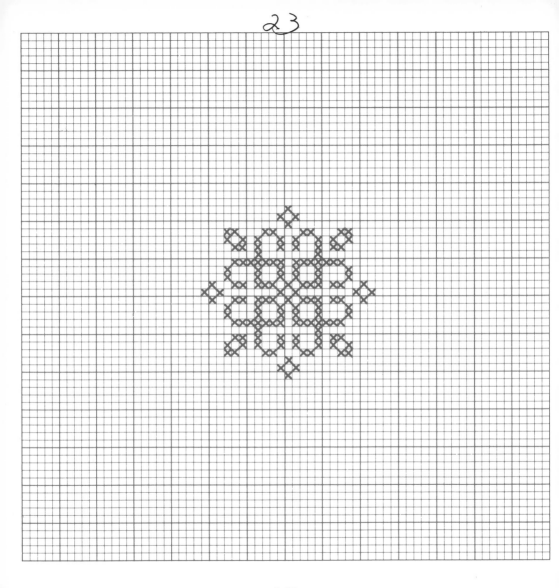

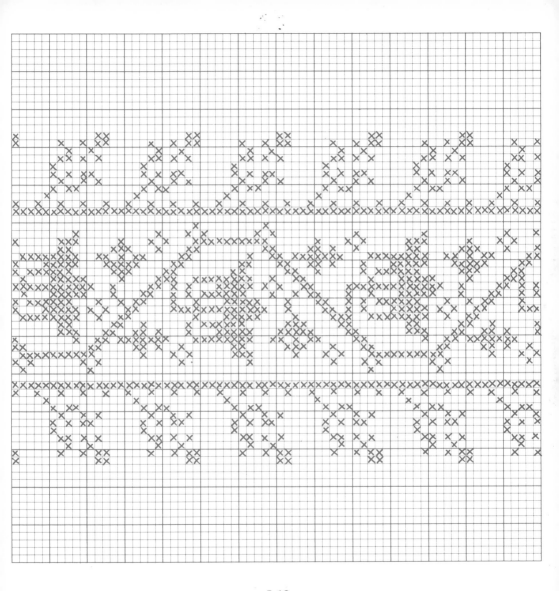

33

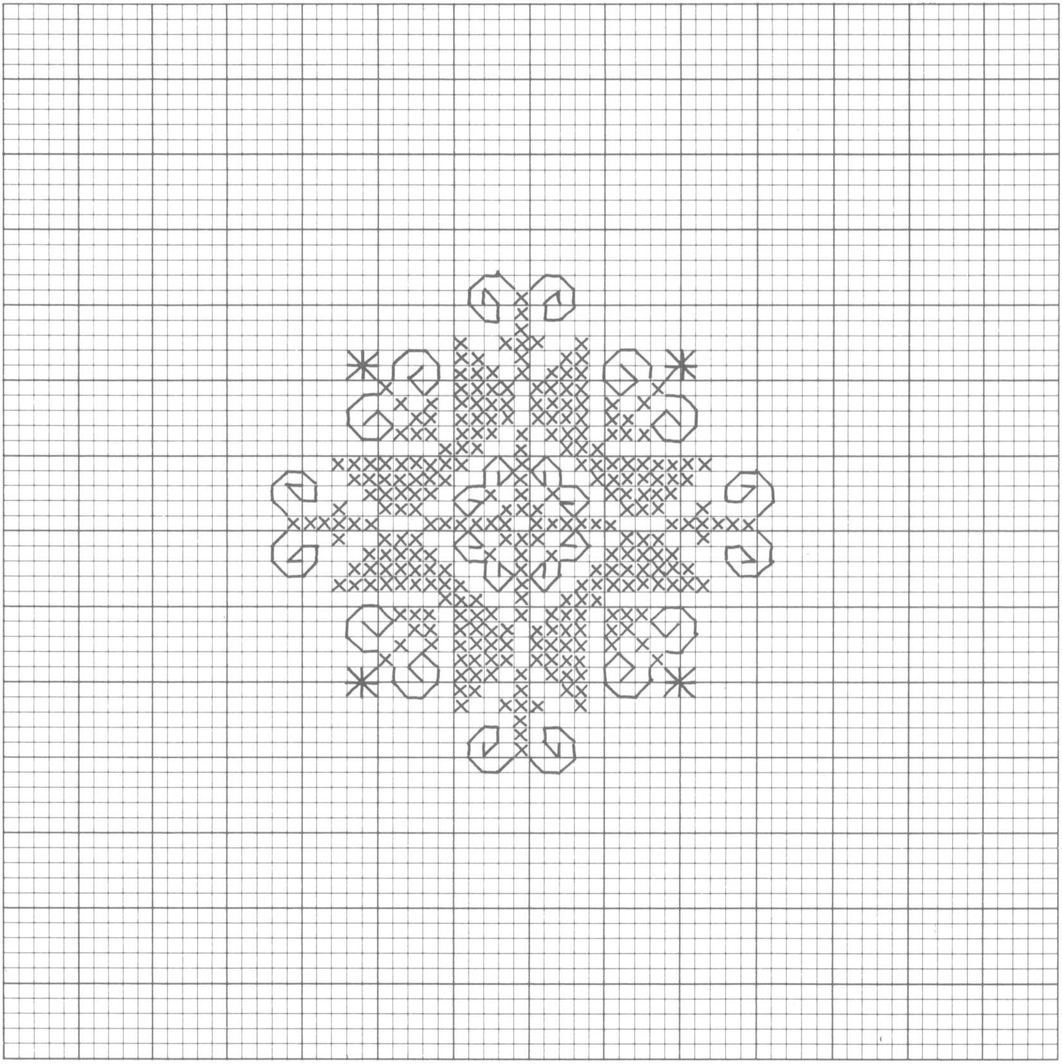

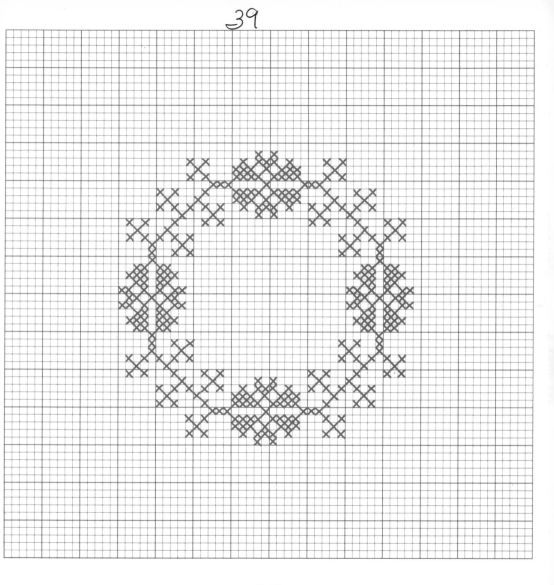

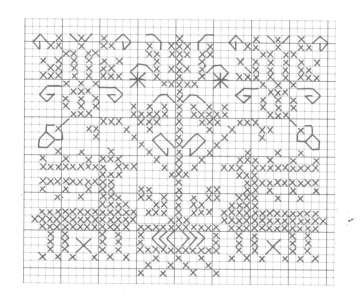

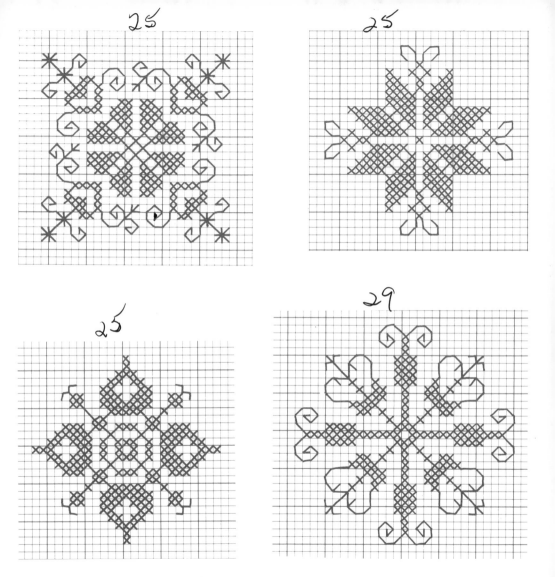